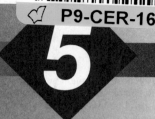

NEW EDITION

5

LADO
ENGLISH SERIES

Robert Lado

Professor of Linguistics Emeritus and Former Dean
School of Languages and Linguistics
Georgetown University

Former Director
English Language Institute
University of Michigan

In collaboration with

JANN HUIZENGA   BERNADETTE SHERIDAN, I.H.M.
JEROME C. FORD   ANNETTE SILVERIO-BORGES

Longman

- look up to => 가르쳐주다
+ looking at (?)
- reliable
- look over
- fly or past.
- build up
=> 강화시키다

Editorial development supervision: Deborah Goldblatt
Editorial development: Deborah Brennan
Editorial/ production supervision: Tunde A. Dewey
Interior design/ page layout: A Good Thing Inc.
Design supervision: Janet Schmid
Manufacturing buyer: Ray Keating

Cover design: Janet Schmid
Cover photograph: Slide Graphics of New England, Inc.

Illustrations by Constance Maltese

Printed in the United States of America

20 19 18 17 16

ISBN   0-13-522327-X

CONTENTS

iv

PREFACE

The new edition of the *Lado English Series* is a complete six-level course in English. Each level is carefully graded and consists of a Student Book, Workbook, Teacher's Edition, and Audio Program. The main objective of the series is to help students understand, speak, read, and write English and to use these four skills for meaningful communications and interaction.

The new *Lado English Series* takes a balanced approach to teaching and learning. It offers a wide variety of techniques and activities—including conversations and discussions, study frames and contextualized grammar exercises, listening and interaction activities, readings and role plays—to help students learn English. The more controlled, structured exercises focus attention on learning the grammatical rules of English, while the freer, open-ended activities offer ways of improving language skills through more creative, spontaneous interaction.

This new edition retains the careful grading, simple presentation, and transparent organization that are classic trademarks of the *Lado English Series*. At the same time, several new features make this edition more modern and easier to use. The revised Student Book format features a larger type size, bigger pages, updated and extended content, and new art. For greater convenience, the Listen section has been moved from the Workbooks to the Student Books. Cassette symbols appear throughout the Student Books to identify recorded material.

The exercises in the six Workbooks correspond to and complement the material covered in the Student Books. They offer additional exercises to help students master the material in each unit and focus on vocabulary, reading, and writing. In this new edition, controlled composition appears in all six Workbooks. In addition, review units with pre- and post-inventory tests are now included at the end of each Workbook.

The Teacher's Editions have been revised and reformatted. The new horizontal page format features clear, concise instructions. For easy reference, these instructions appear in single columns on each page of the Teacher's Edition and face a nearly full-size reproduction of the corresponding page from the Student Book. The answers to all the exercises are given together with the reproduced page. New vocabulary presented in the unit is listed at the beginning of each section. This is followed by a concise explanation of how to teach the section. Suggestions for games are also given, so that students have the opportunity to use English in less formal situations. Answers to all Workbook exercises can be found in an answer key at the back of the Teacher's Edition.

An Audio Program for each level consists of five cassettes corresponding to each Student Book. The program gives students the opportunity to listen to native speech, and can be used outside of class to provide extra speaking and listening practice.

By offering a combination of controlled and open-ended exercises and activities, Student Book 5 helps students achieve grammatical correctness and build effective communication skills. The first two sections of each unit are more controlled: Students practice a dialogue in the opening Conversation section, then answer a series of questions in the Answer and Discuss section that follows. Some of these questions allow students to check their comprehension of the dialogue, while others encourage them to talk about their own experiences. In the new Interaction section that comes next, role-playing and discussion activities, based on the opening dialogue, allow students to generate their own conversational exchanges. Moreover, this section allows students to use English more naturally and functionally before they focus on particular language structures in the Study and Practice sections that follow. Thus, students work with both the function (use) and the grammatical form (structure) of English.

Student Book 5 has ten units. These units are divided into sections with clear headings that indicate the purpose of the sections: Conversation, Answer and Discuss, Interaction, Study, Practice, Listen, Read, Phrasal Verbs, Think and Speak, Vocabulary Expansion, and Pronounce. Following are guidelines for presenting the material in each unit.

Each unit opens with a **Conversation** that introduces the new material in a communicative setting. A picture and background statement (see Teacher's Edition) help to set the context. Intonation lines show the rise and fall of the voice. They represent the four intonation levels of English: low, mid, high, and extra high. A dot on the intonation line indicates the principal stress in each sentence.

- Describe the situation while students look at the picture.
- Explain any new or unfamiliar vocabulary or structures.
- Read the conversation while students follow along in their books.
- Assign each role to a part of the class. Read the conversation and have the students repeat the lines that correspond to their roles.
- Assign each role to an individual student. Read the conversation and have the students repeat the lines that correspond to their roles.
- Divide the class into pairs or small groups and have the students practice the conversation.
- Ask a group to present the conversation in front of the class.

An **Answer and Discuss** section follows each conversation and features two types of questions. Comprehension questions allow students to check their understanding of factual information presented in the dialogue. Open-ended questions give students an opportunity to talk about themselves and relate their own experiences to topics in the dialogue.

- Read each question aloud, or call on students to volunteer.
- Allow the students time to respond to each question before you call for an answer. This will ensure that the whole class is working on the answers.
- If students fail to answer appropriately, give them time to check the answer and try again.
- Acknowledge correct answers.

In the **Interaction** sections, students adapt the opening conversation to new situations in role-playing and discussion activities. These activities encourage personal expression and creativity by giving students a chance to relate the opening dialogues to their own lives. For the role-playing activities, follow this standard procedure:

- Read the roles to the students, presenting any vocabulary that they may need.
- Divide the class into pairs and have each pair prepare a dialogue that could take place in the situation. You may wish to have the students write a "script."
- Call on several pairs of students to act out their dialogues in front of the class.

The **Study** sections present grammatical structures in a clear, graphic way. Study frames have been redone in the new edition, with boxes, connecting lines, and illustrations updated to make the grammatical relationships clearer.

- Read the examples while students follow along in their books.
- Explain the structure(s), using the example sentences and illustrations.
- Give further examples of the structure to ensure student comprehension.

A **Practice** section follows each Study frame. This section contains exercises which allow students to use the target grammar in meaningful contexts. Many exercises include an additional application step (see Teacher's edition), in which students personalize the structures by giving information about themselves.

- Explain any new or unfamiliar vocabulary.
- Present the example to the class. Check for comprehension.
- Have students do the exercises.

The **Listen** section contains exercises that are similar to those on standardized listening–proficiency tests. The exercises, which require students to listen to sentences or dialogues and then check the correct choices, can be used for listening practice or for listening-comprehension tests. All exercises are included on the audio cassettes available for each level of the series.

- If you are using the exercises for listening practice, read (or play) each item twice and let the students respond.
- If you are using them for tests, read or play the items only once.

- After students have completed each exercise, write the correct responses on the board so that they can check their work.

The **Read** section contains a wide range of authentic selections, from the short story to the magazine-style biography. Questions follow each reading to check comprehension and stimulate discussion. Reading has become increasingly emphasized as a language skill as students have worked through the series.

- Explain any new or unfamiliar vocabulary.
- Have the students read the text silently, using the illustration (if there is one) to help them understand the content.
- Ask students to work in pairs and ask and answer the questions. If students do not agree on an answer, have them return to the reading passage to resolve their disagreement.

The **Phrasal Verbs** section presents high-frequency two-word and three-word verbs in contextualized paragraphs that help students understand their meaning. A **Practice** section, similar to those following the Study sections, follows each presentation of Phrasal Verbs.

- Read the paragraph aloud as the students follow in their books.
- Go over the definition of each phrasal verb at the bottom of the Study frame.
- To check student comprehension, have the students create original sentences using the phrasal verbs.

The **Think and Speak** section gives students another opportunity to use English in a less-controlled, more communicative way. The pictures in this section encourage students to use new structures and vocabulary freely and creatively.

- Ask students to look at and think about the illustrations. Help them with vocabulary if necessary.
- Have students talk about the illustrations, preferably in pairs or small groups.
- Encourage students to relate their own experiences to the situation(s) if appropriate.

The **Vocabulary Expansion** section presents a pair or group of common prefixes and suffixes. (First, words containing the prefixes and suffixes are used in contextualized paragraphs.) Then the words are broken down into their components, and the prefixes and suffixes are defined. Each Vocabulary Expansion section is followed by a **Practice** section.

- Read the paragraphs aloud as the students follow in their books.
- Go over the diagrams showing the formation of the words and read aloud the rules at the bottom of the Study frame.
- Have the students create original sentences using the prefixed or suffixed words.

The **Pronounce** sections focus on particular elements of pronunciation that may cause problems in understanding and speaking English. These sections not only treat all of the phonemes of English, but also deal with consonant clusters and other aspects of pronunciation unique to English spelling, stress, and intonation. In many cases, facial diagrams illustrate the articulation of phonemes, and in the intermediate and advanced levels, students practice the featured sounds in the larger context of a paragraph. Some of the Pronounce sections in this edition also include a proverb illustrating the key sounds.

- Point out the key sounds and the facial diagram (if there is one).
- Pronounce the words (or play the appropriate cassette) and have the students practice saying them.
- To present the paragraphs, ask the students first to say each of the sentences individually; then have them read aloud the entire paragraph.

This new edition offers a complete and balanced program for teaching and learning the structures and functions of English. Hopefully, the new features and design will make the series even more appealing, convenient, and effective for promoting learning and communication.

Robert Lado
Washington, D.C.

UNIT 1

CONVERSATION

Deciding between Work and Entertainment

Gary and Alice are in the same history class at the university. Today the university baseball team has an exciting game. Gary wants to go. Alice would rather stay home and read a chapter in her history book.

GARY: Let's go to the baseball game.

ALICE: I'd love to, but I can't. It's because of the history exam. I still have another chapter to read.

1

2

GARY: So do I. But the exam isn't until next week. You'll have enough time to read it this weekend.

ALICE: I don't like to put things off until the last minute. It makes me too nervous.

GARY: But with history, it's better to put off studying until just before the exam. That way you don't forget the names and dates.

ALICE: That may be good enough for you, but I have to study every day to keep up.

GARY: You shouldn't study all the time. That's why you're always so nervous. Besides, this is the best game of the season.

ALICE: Isn't it more important to get a good grade on the exam than to see the game?

GARY: I'll pass the exam. I always work best under pressure.

Answer and Discuss

1. Who wants to go to the baseball game?
2. Why can't Alice go?
3. Why doesn't Alice like to put things off until the last minute?

4. Why does Gary put off studying history until just before the exam?
5. What does Alice have to do to keep up?
6. Why does Gary think Alice should go to the game? Give two reasons.
7. What does Alice think is more important?
8. How does Gary work best?
9. Who do you agree with, Alice or Gary? Why?
10. Do you ever put things off? Do you work well under pressure?

INTERACTION

A. Read the following situation. Then, with a partner, play one of the roles listed.

A rock star is going to give a concert in your town tonight. She has never been here before and will be here only tonight.

1. You want a classmate to go to the concert with you, but he or she wants to study English tonight instead. You think that it's bad to study all the time. Your friend will have enough time to study this weekend. Also, the concert is going to be a very exciting one.
2. Your classmate wants you to go to a rock concert with him or her. You're planning to study your English lesson tonight. You like to study a little every day to keep up with the class. Also, there's going to be an English exam next week.

B. Discuss the following paragraph with a partner or with the class.

Some people like to get up early in the morning, eat a good breakfast, and spend a lot of time getting dressed before they go to work or school. They don't like to rush. Other people prefer to sleep late and get up only a half hour before they have to leave. They usually don't have breakfast—just a cup of tea or coffee. They think it's wasteful to spend a lot of time getting ready in the morning. Do you usually get up early or late? Why?

STUDY 1

The expression **because of**: *It's because of the history exam.*

Notice the use of **because of**.

Why does the Diaz family like Florida?
Because the weather is warm.

| **Because of** | the weather.

Why does Mr. Diaz like Florida?
Because the fishing is good.

| **Because of** | the fishing.

Why does Mrs. Diaz like to drive to Florida?
Because the highways are excellent.

| **Because of** | the excellent highways.

Use **because of** before a noun or noun phrase. Include an appropriate adjective when necessary to make the meaning clear.

Because of the **excellent** highways.

 # PRACTICE

A. Ask a question about the first statement using *why*. Use *because of* + a noun to answer the question.

EX.   Mr. and Mrs. Murphy are staying at their son Al's house in Florida during their vacation. They miss their grandchildren.
  ▷   **Why are Mr. and Mrs. Murphy staying at their son Al's house in Florida during their vacation?**
       Because of their grandchildren.

1.   Mr. Murphy caught a cold before their vacation. The weather was very cold.
  ▷

2. He can't smell the flowers in his son's garden. He has a cold.
▷

3. Mrs. Murphy doesn't like to work in the garden. She hates the bugs.
▷

4. The Murphys like Florida. The climate is pleasant.
▷

5. They don't like Al's cooking. He uses a lot of salt.
▷

B. Answer the questions according to the pictures. Use *because of* + a noun.

EX. Why didn't you go sailing yesterday?
Because of the weather.
It was raining.

1. Why can't Martha have dinner with us?

_____

She's had a bad cold all week.

2. Why did you leave the beach so early?

_____

It was blowing very hard.

3. Why won't you come in?

_____

I'm afraid of it.

4. Why don't you buy those shoes?

_____

They're very expensive.

$100⁰⁰

[handwritten: A: why are you hurrying?]
[handwritten: B: I catch the bus]
[handwritten: —Because I need to catch the bus.]

STUDY 2

[handwritten: ＊ because of 다음에 (n)이 나온다]
[handwritten: 주어+ (EX)]
[handwritten: because of the bus]

To infinitive phrase of purpose: *[handwritten: 목적·의지]*
I have to study every day to keep up.

Notice the meaning and use of the **to** infinitive.

Why are you hurrying?

[handwritten: A: why do you like florida?]

| **To catch** | the bus.

[handwritten: 동사원형 infinitive — purpose.]

Where are you going?

[handwritten: B: because of the weather.]

To the airport | **to meet** | Mary Ann.

When do you have to leave?

[handwritten: why와 born cm because 4]
[handwritten: to infinitive 6]

I have to leave at 8:15 | **to get** | there by 9:00.

Why is she coming?

To attend | a convention.

Use the **to** infinitive to express purpose or reason. Put the **to**
infinitive at the beginning of short answers.

Why are you going by bus?
To save money.

PRACTICE

[handwritten: 질문에 근거임]

**Answer the questions according to the pictures. First give a short
answer using the *to* infinitive. Then answer with a complete sentence.**

EX. Why does Sandra drive downtown
after work?
▷ **To go to a community college.
She drives downtown after work
to go to a community college.**

COMMUNITY
COLLEGE

1. **Why is she going to school at night?**

▷ To learn how to repair cars.

She's going to school at night to learn how to repair cars.

2. **Why does she read the ads in the paper?**

▷ To look for a find job. (real job)

She reads the ads in the paper to look for a job.

3. **Why does she work so many hours now?**

▷

4. **Why is she saving money?**

▷

5. **Why is she staying up late?**

▷

STUDY 3

Very/too: *It makes me too nervous.*

Notice the use of **very** and **too**. 정확 확이 토다.

WITH ADJECTIVES:

It was | **very** windy, | but it wasn't | **too** windy | to swim.
Some " _more_ "

The water was | **very** cold, | but it wasn't | **too** cold | for me.

WITH ADVERBS:

He drives | **very** well, | but he drives | **too** fast | for me.

We woke up | **very** early, | but arrived at the station | **too** late.

Very means "to a high degree."
Too means "to an excessive degree."
Use **very** and **too** before adjectives and adverbs.

PRACTICE

Answer the questions using *very* or *too*.

EX. I hear you went to the rally on the environment in Washington, D.C. last weekend. How was it?
Very well organized. Everything went smoothly.

1. Did many people come from California?
No. It was ___too___ far away. Few Californians came.

2. Was the weather cold?
Yes. _very_ cold. But everyone wore warm clothes.

3. Did the speaker talk for a long time?
Yes. _too_ long. People were talking and moving around.

4. Could all the marchers stand on the steps of the Capitol?
No. There were _too_ many. They didn't fit on the steps.

5. Was the rally successful?
Yes. _very_ successful. It was on all the news shows.

STUDY 4

Enough: *You'll have enough time to read it this weekend.*

Notice the meaning and use of **enough**.

WITH ADJECTIVES:

Is this coat | large **enough** | for you?

WITH ADVERBS:

Yes, it fits | well **enough**. |

WITH NOUNS:

Does it have | **enough** pockets? | Yes, it has | **enough** | (pockets).

Enough means "adequate or sufficient."
Use **enough** after adjectives and adverbs and before nouns.
In short answers with **enough,** you may omit the noun, but not an
adjective or adverb.

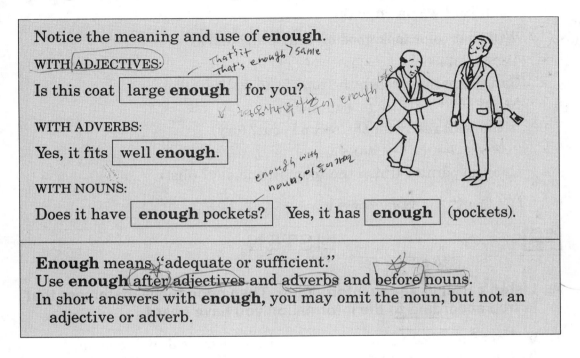

PRACTICE

A. Answer the questions using *enough* and the cues.

EX. Why is Lily tired? (sleep)
▷ **Because she didn't get enough sleep.**

1. Why didn't Lily eat her breakfast? (time)
▷

2. Why didn't she drive to work? (gas)
▷

3. Why didn't she take a taxi to work? (money)
▷

4. Why didn't she get on the bus? (change)
▷
Because She didn't have enough change.

adjective → always to beer bong (handwritten)

B. Give negative short responses to these questions using the cues and *enough*.

EX.   Is winter a good time to swim? (warm)
▷   **No, it isn't warm enough.**

1.   Will that color look good on that wall? (dark)
▷   *No, it won't be dark enough.*

2.   Can the painter reach the top of the wall? (tall)
▷   *No, he can't. He isn't tall enough*

3.   Is the wall ready for the second coat? (dry)
▷   *No, it isn't dry enough.*

4.   Can the painter finish the room in one day? (fast)
▷   *No, he isn't fast enough.*

LISTEN

A. Listen carefully to the information. Then choose the statement that is true according to the information you have heard.

1.   a. I get up at 7:00 now.
   b. I get up at 7:30 now.
   c. I get up at 6:30 now.

2.   a. Norma paid $50.
   b. Norma paid $15.
   c. Norma paid $25.

3.   a. Karen bought a store.
   b. Karen bought a sailboat.
   c. Karen sold a sailboat.

4.   a. Ken is June's cousin.
   b. Ken is June's brother.
   c. Ken is June's friend.

5.   a. We can pay for the house.
   b. We bought a house.
   c. We can't buy the house.

6.   a. We should leave at 7:00.
   b. The play starts at 7:00.
   c. We should leave at 7:30.

B. Listen carefully to the information. Then choose the correct answer.

1.   a. Next week.
   b. Next weekend.
   c. This weekend.

2.   a. One hour and 15 minutes.
   b. One half-hour.
   c. Forty-five minutes.

3.   a. Dallas.
   b. Washington.
   c. New York.

4.   a. Two blocks.
   b. Three blocks.
   c. Five blocks.

READ

Procrastination

The verb *procrastinate* comes from the Latin *procrastinare,* which means "to postpone until tomorrow." To procrastinate, then, is to delay doing something until some future time. A procrastinator is someone who is always putting off what he or she should be doing right now.

Those of us who have a tendency toward procrastination know that it is a terrible habit. Every day, we tell ourselves that we must start doing things immediately. Every day, we postpone our work, miss deadlines, and break promises. Because we always procrastinate, we are always trying to catch up. We are always doing yesterday's jobs today, and today's jobs tomorrow.

There are people who rarely procrastinate. They are highly efficient and well organized. They seem to get everything done on time. I suspect that they never leave home in the morning before they make the bed, never go to sleep at night before they finish their work, and are never late for appointments. As a result, they are probably always one step ahead of you and me.

Maybe the way to overcome procrastination is to change our habits gradually. We can start with a daily schedule of the things we need to accomplish. But let's be reasonable. We shouldn't crowd the list with too many tasks. We should be realistic about what we can do. Especially in the beginning, we should be lenient with ourselves. After all, if we fail at the start, we will get discouraged and go right back to our old habits.

Answer and Discuss

1. What is a procrastinator?
2. What are some of the habits of a procrastinator?
3. How is a well-organized person different from a procrastinator?
4. Is it easy to stop procrastinating? Give reasons.
5. How can we overcome the habit of putting things off?
6. Why should we be lenient with ourselves in the beginning?
7. Do you ever procrastinate? What things do you put off?

PHRASAL VERBS 1

Call up, get over, go over, put off, turn off, turn on

Notice the difference in meaning between **put** and **put off**.
I **put** my car in a neighbor's garage.
I'm a procrastinator. I **put off** my work as long as possible.

Put off is a phrasal verb consisting of a verb and a particle. The meaning of phrasal verbs is often idiomatic; that is, the meaning of the combination is different from the meaning of the individual words.

Notice the meaning of these phrasal verbs.
Alice doesn't like to **put** things **off** until the last minute.
She studies every day and **goes over** her class notes regularly.
She works even when she is **getting over** a cold or the flu.
Gary **puts off** studying until just before the exam.
When he needs help with his work, he **calls** Alice **up.**
Gary **turns on** the radio and listens to music when he studies.
If the radio is on, Alice **turns it off** before she begins to work.

Call up means "telephone."
Get over means "recover from" (an illness).
Go over means "review" (something).
Put off means "delay" (something).
Turn off means "stop the flow of" (electricity, gas, water).
Turn on means "start the flow of" (electricity, gas, water).

*(run into = crash (衝突(①)) = meet by chane

PRACTICE

Complete the sentences using the correct form of an appropriate verb from the following list.

call	get	go	put	turn
call up	get over	go over	put off	turn off

Last winter, Bernard caught a cold, and he stayed in bed for a whole week to _____ it. When he _____ to school again on Monday, his history teacher announced that there would be a test that Friday. Bernard immediately borrowed notes from his friend Martha, _____ them in his briefcase, and went to the library to photocopy them. He had to _____ Martha several times to ask questions about them. He studied every night and never _____ his light before midnight. He didn't _____ the television or the radio for the entire week. He did nothing but read the textbook and _____ the notes. He __*got*__ a very good grade on the test that week. Bernard says, "Never __*put off*__ until tomorrow what you can do today." Bernard's friends __*call*__ him "Lucky" because he gets good grades, but Bernard knows that it's more than just luck.

PHRASAL VERBS 2

Separable phrasal verbs

Notice the position of the direct object with these phrasal verbs.

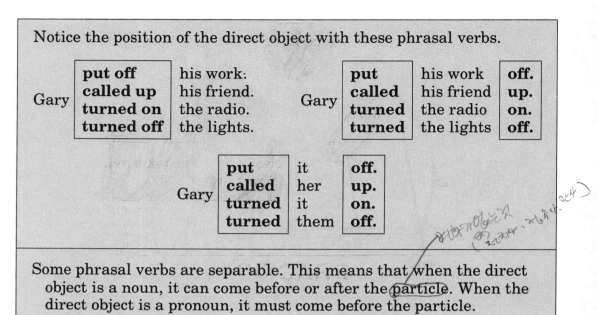

Some phrasal verbs are separable. This means that when the direct object is a noun, it can come before or after the particle. When the direct object is a pronoun, it must come before the particle.

PRACTICE

Say each sentence two other ways, first using the noun and then the pronoun.

EX. He called up his aunt.
▷ **He called his aunt up.**
He called her up.

1. She put off her work.
▷

2. Please take off your shoes.
▷

3. Try on these slippers.
▷

4. Put on this hat.
▷

5. Did you turn on the light?
▷

6. Leave out the details.
▷

7. Turn off the radio.
▷

PHRASAL VERBS 3

Nonseparable phrasal verbs

Notice the position of the direct object with these verbs.

She	**got over**	her cold.	She	**got over**	it.
I	**went over**	the homework.	I	**went over**	it.
We	**looked into**	the report.	We	**looked into**	it.

Many phrasal verbs are nonseparable; that is, the verb and the particle cannot be separated by a direct object.

PRACTICE

A bicycle ran into Norma as she was crossing the street. Answer these questions affirmatively using pronouns.

EX. Did the bicycle run into Norma?
▷ **Yes, it ran into her.**

1. Did Norma get over the shock?
▷

2. Did Norma go over the details with the police?
▷

3. Will the police look into the accident?
▷

4. Will the director go over your report in detail?
▷

5. Do bicycles often run into people?
▷

THINK AND SPEAK

What is happening in this picture? How are Rosa and Patrick different? Who do you identify with more? Why?

VOCABULARY EXPANSION

The prefixes **mis-** and **re-**

Notice the meaning and formation of these words.

	use	**misuse**
mis-	+ spell =	**misspell**
	read	**misread**

He used the word wrong. He **misused** the word.
He spelled the word wrong. He **misspelled** the word.
He read the word wrong. He **misread** the word.

	use	**reuse**
re-	+ read =	**reread**
	write	**rewrite**

She used the bag again. She **reused** the bag.
She read the contract again. She **reread** the contract.
She wrote the letter again. She **rewrote** the letter.

The prefix **mis-** adds the meaning "in the wrong way."
The prefix **re-** adds the meaning "again" or "once more."

PRACTICE

Complete the story by filling in the prefix *mis-* or *re-* in the blanks.

Mr. Keith works in the personnel department of a large company. Yesterday a long-time employee came to his office. He didn't recognize her. He _____took her for a visitor. Finally, he realized that she was an employee, but he _____pronounced her name. The employee explained that she had applied for a leave of absence. Mr. Keith told her that he had _____placed her application and that she should _____apply. He wrote her name at the top of a new form. Unfortunately, he _____spelled her name, so he had to erase it and _____write it. While she was filling out the form, he started to _____arrange his papers, and he _____placed the employee's file.

PRONOUNCE: [ay]

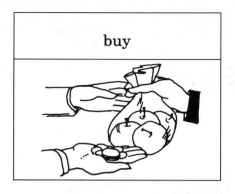

buy

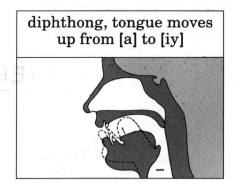

diphthong, tongue moves
up from [a] to [iy]

A. Repeat the following words.

by	high	life	pipe	why
child	I'm	like	right	wife
five	knife	nine	time	wine

B. On a separate sheet of paper, write the numbers of words that have the sound [ay] as in *buy*.

1. ride	3. say	5. sit	7. shy	9. nine
2. child	4. high	6. eye	8. make	10. pin

C. Listen to this paragraph. Repeat each sentence after the speaker.

Guy and I are going to ride our bicycles to the beach on Friday. It's a nice, quiet place with white sand and wild birds. Would you like to ride with us?

CONVERSATION

Lost and Found

Carlos and Nancy are walking down a busy city street. Suddenly, Carlos sees a wallet on the ground. He <u>picks it up to</u> look at it.

CARLOS: Look what I found! A wallet with forty dollars in it.

NANCY: Does it have the owner's name and address inside?

CARLOS: Let me see. There's a name—Marilyn Jackson—but no address.

19

NANCY: Good! Then you can keep it.

CARLOS: Maybe I should take it to the police. What if the owner really needs the money?

NANCY: So what? In a big city like this, you can't give it back without an address, and the police can't, either. Just keep it.

CARLOS: No—I'll put an ad in the paper.

NANCY: That's ridiculous! It's only forty dollars, and an ad is expensive.

WOMAN: Excuse me. Did anybody see a wallet around here? I lost mine a little while ago.

CARLOS: What's your name?

WOMAN: Marilyn Jackson.

CARLOS: Great! Here it is.

WOMAN: Thank you so much. I really appreciate this, and my husband will, too. Without this money, we couldn't buy groceries this week.

Answer and Discuss

1. What did Carlos find?
2. Whose wallet is it? What is the owner's address?
3. Why does Nancy say that Carlos can keep it?
4. Why doesn't she think that he should take it to the police?
5. How does Carlos hope to find the owner?
6. What does Nancy think is ridiculous?
7. How does Carlos know that the wallet is hers?
8. What do you do when you find something on the street?
9. Tell the story as if you were Carlos.
10. Tell the story as if you were Nancy.

INTERACTION

Read the following ads for lost items. Then, with a partner, choose one of the items below and play one of the roles listed.

LOST AND FOUND		
KEYS—found on Fifth Ave. near 23rd on 4/23. Call 466-1114.	BRIEFCASE—found 4/25 in Wall St. area. Call 321-9614.	BRACELET—silver, found on X28 bus. 445-1681.
WRISTWATCH—found 4/29 in cab. 466-6161.	WALLET—found on Elm Street 4/19. 321-4401.	RING—gold, found in women's room at Astor Cinema. 988-2351.

1. Imagine that you have found the item in the ad. Write down a description of the item and the details of when and where you found it. When your partner calls (a person who has lost this or a similar item), ask questions about the item to see if he or she can identify it.
2. Imagine you have lost the item. "Call" the number listed in the ad. (Your partner will answer.) Describe the item you lost to see if it is the one advertised.

*He ran a marathon. and I did too
and so did I.*

main verb

STUDY 1

And...too connecting two affirmative statements:
I really appreciate this, and my husband will, too.

Notice the use of **and...too**.

John is from Texas. I'm from Texas.

John is from Texas, and I am, too.

He lives in Dallas. I live in Dallas.

He lives in Dallas, and I do, too.

me too 는 informal
I do too

He can speak Spanish. I can speak Spanish.

He can speak Spanish, and I can, too.

*You are from Icorea
→ I am from too*
*she wear earing
and I do too*

He's lived there for years. I've lived there for years.

has

He's lived there for years, and I have, too.

He will — and I will too

Use **and...too** to connect two affirmative sentences. You can
complete the second sentence with the uncontracted form of the
auxiliary (**am, do, can, have,** etc.) + **too** to avoid repeating
information.

A different pattern with the same meaning is given below. Notice
that the subject and verb are inverted. Both patterns are
acceptable and commonly used.

John is from Texas, **and so am I.**
He lives in Dallas, **and so do I.**

Aux
She will go to France and I will too.

You should study and I should too

I listen to music (simple present sentence는 Aux가 X)
main verb   and she does too.
and so does she.

(handwritten margin notes)
same meaning & so는 밥이 do 가능해 너무 앞에 subject
subs → nm 봐   can
do   does
can   has
will
have

PRACTICE

Margaret and Leo both work at a stationery store. They have a lot in common. Add another sentence to each of the following, using *and* ... *too* and the cue in parentheses.

EX.   Margaret is a salesperson. (Leo)
▷   **Margaret is a salesperson, and Leo is, too.**

1.   Leo has worked at this store for a long time. (Margaret)
▷   *Leo has worked at this store for a long time, and Margaret has too.*

2.   Leo sells stationery. (Margaret)
▷   *Leo sells stationery and margaret does too*

3.   Margaret smiles at the customers. (Leo)
▷   *Margaret smiles at the customers and leo does too*

4.   Leo can wrap packages well. (Margaret)
▷   *Leo can wrap packages well and margaret can too*

5.   Margaret counts money carefully. (Leo)
▷   *Margaret counts money carefully and Leo does too*

6.   They both will work late tonight. (the other salespeople)
▷   *They both will work late tonight and the other salespeople will too*

7.   Leo will take the bus home. (Margaret)
▷   *Leo will take the bus home and Margaret will too*

8.   Margaret is very tired. (Leo)
▷   *Margaret is very tired and so is Leo*

STUDY 2

And...either connecting two negative statements:
You can't give it back, and the police can't, either.

Notice the use of **and...either.**

Simon isn't a swimmer. I'm not a swimmer.

Simon isn't a swimmer, | **and I'm not, either.** |

He's never taken lessons. I've never taken lessons.

He's never taken lessons, | **and I haven't, either.** |

He doesn't dive. I don't dive.

He doesn't dive, | **and I don't, either.** |

He can't float. I can't float.

He can't float, | **and I can't, either.** |

Use **and...either** to connect two negative statements. You can complete the second sentence simply with the negative form of the auxiliary + **either** to avoid repeating information, as above.

A different pattern with the same meaning is given below, using **neither** in place of **not either**. Notice that the subject and verb are inverted. Both patterns are acceptable and commonly used.

Simon isn't a swimmer, **and neither am I.**
He doesn't dive, **and neither do I.**

PRACTICE

Both Wing and Sylvia have excellent characters. Answer the questions using the *and...either* pattern. First give a short answer; then give a longer statement as in the example.

EX. Wing doesn't tell lies. What about Sylvia?
▷ **Sylvia doesn't either.**
Wing doesn't tell lies, and Sylvia doesn't, either.

1. Sylvia has never been disloyal to a friend. What about Wing?
▷ ~~Wing doesn't~~ *hasn't* either
   ~~Sylvia doesn't~~ *has never been disloyal to a friend and wing ~~doesn't~~ either* *hasn't*

2. Wing doesn't waste time. What about Sylvia?
▷ *Sylvia doesn't either. Wing doesn't waste time. and sylvia desn't, either.*

3. Sylvia doesn't break promises. What about Wing?
▷ *whing doesn't either.*
   Sylvia doesn't break promises and wing doesn't, either.

4. Wing is never dishonest. What about Sylvia?
▷ *sylvia isn't either.*
   Wing is never dishonest, and sylvia isn't either.

5. Sylvia has never been unkind to anyone. What about Wing?
▷ *wing hasn't either. (= neither has wing) and*
   sylvia has never been unkind to anyone. wing hasn't, either.

6. Wing doesn't hold grudges. What about Sylvia?
▷ *sylvia doesn't either*   *he is hold grudes*
   Wing doesn't hold grudges. and sylvia doesn't ettha.
   stay angry

STUDY 3

But connecting an affirmative and a negative statement:
Most wallets have an address inside, but this one doesn't.

Notice the use of **but**.

Karen is at the office. The other employees aren't at the office.

Karen is at the office, | **but the other employees aren't.**

They don't like to work late. Karen likes to work late.

They don't like to work late, | **but Karen does.**

They've already gone home. Karen hasn't gone home yet.

They've already gone home, | **but Karen hasn't**.

Karen could leave earlier. Karen doesn't want to leave earlier.

Karen could leave earlier, | **but she doesn't want to**.

Use **but** to connect an affirmative and a negative sentence. You can complete the second sentence simply with an auxiliary or a shortened form of the sentence to avoid repeating information.

PRACTICE

Add another sentence to each of the following, using *but* and the cue in parentheses.

EX. Ecuador sells bananas. (Chile)
  ▷ **Ecuador sells bananas, but Chile doesn't.**

  Panama doesn't have a ski industry. (Switzerland)
  ▷ **Panama doesn't have a ski industry, but Switzerland does.**

1. Venezuela doesn't import oil. (France)
   ▷ *venezuela doesnt import oil but France does.*

2. Brazil exported millions of tons of coffee last year. (Canada)
   ▷ *Brazil exported millions of tons of coffee last year but canada*

3. Argentina is a producer of olive oil. (England)
   ▷ *Argentina is a producer of olive oil but England doesn't,* ~~doesn't~~ *isn't didn't*

4. Panama doesn't export cars. (Japan)
   ▷ *Panama doesn't export cars but Japan does.*

ex) He plays soccer I don't play soccer

He plays soccer, but I don't.

LISTEN

Listen carefully to the information. Then choose the statement that is true according to the information you have heard.

1. a. She has a job now.   *I can't*
   b. She didn't take the job.
   c. She didn't think about the job.

2. a. She didn't buy anything.
   b. She bought some bread.
   c. She bought some doughnuts.

3. a. She's a good music student.
   b. She's a poor music student.
   c. She's a music teacher.

4. a. I didn't tell Claudia to buy stamps for me.
   b. Claudia didn't buy the stamps.
   c. Claudia bought the stamps.

5. a. He didn't want to sing, but he did.
   b. He wanted to sing, but he didn't.
   c. He didn't want to sing, and he didn't.

6. a. Carmen must pay me $40.
   b. Carmen must pay me $9.
   c. Carmen must pay me $8.

READ

Interpreting Your Dreams

We don't all remember our dreams, but experts agree that we all dream about 25 percent of the time we are asleep. Dreams can be very short or as long as an hour. They can be strange, amusing, frightening, or just ordinary. Whatever kind of dream we have, it carries a message from the subconscious mind.

Sometimes other people can see that we are dreaming. Rapid eye movements (REMs) occur during the deepest level of sleep. When people are awakened in the middle of one of these periods of sleep, they almost always report vivid dreams. Some scientists think that the eyes move as they do at these times because the eyes are watching the dream activity. A woman whose eyes moved back and forth during sleep said later that she had been dreaming about a tennis match.

If you have trouble recalling your dreams, try the following:

• Every night before going to sleep, tell yourself that you will remember your dreams.

• Keep a pen and paper by your bedside. As soon as you wake up, write down everything you can remember.

• Since your last dream usually begins right before your normal waking hour, set your alarm to ring a few minutes earlier. In this way, you might wake up in the middle of a dream.

As you learn to remember your dreams, you will have fun with them, and you may understand yourself better, too. First, try a literal interpretation of the dream. Then see what hidden meaning may also be in it. The following are two common dream themes and their possible meanings.

• You want to talk to someone. The telephone rings. You answer it, but there is no one at the other end. You may be feeling rejected by a friend.

• You are walking through dark woods, and you lose your way. You may be insecure about some aspect of your life.

If you have a problem that you have been unable to solve, look for an answer in your dreams. Before you fall asleep, tell yourself that you will know the solution when you wake up. Even though this method may not work at first, keep trying. Some morning when you least expect it, you may wake up with the solution.

Answer and Discuss

1. Does everyone dream? How much?
2. Where do dreams originate?
3. What are REMs? When do they occur? What is one possible explanation for them?
4. Do you have trouble remembering your dreams?
5. How can you recall your dreams more easily?
6. What kind of dream interpretation should you try first?
7. Have you had either of the dreams mentioned in the article? Tell about it.
8. According to the article, can you look for a solution to a problem in your sleep? How?
9. Tell the class about a recent dream you've had.
10. Do you believe in dream interpretation? Give reasons.

PHRASAL VERBS

Count on, give back, and give in (to)

Notice the meaning of these phrasal verbs.

Did Carlos **give** the wallet **back** to the owner?
  Yes. He **gave** it **back**.

Can you **count on** Carlos to do the right thing?
  Yes. You can always **count on** him to do the right thing.

Did Carlos **give in to** the temptation to keep the wallet?
  No. He didn't **give in**.

Count on (nonseparable) means "depend on."
Give back (separable) means "return" (something).
Give in means "submit, surrender." It does not take a direct object.
  However, when **to** is added, it does take a direct object. **Give in to**
  is nonseparable.

PRACTICE

Complete the sentences with the correct form of an appropriate verb from the following list.

count	give	give in
count on	give back	give in to

1. Paul wanted me to have a piece of chocolate cake, but I didn't
   _____ the temptation.
2. Paul had three pieces of cake. I know because I _____ them.
3. May helped me wash the windows; I can always _____ her.
4. I _____ May a scarf for her birthday.
5. I lent Bertha my dictionary last week, and she hasn't _____ it
   _____ yet.
6. I didn't want to lend it to her, but she asked me for it so often that I
   finally _____ .

THINK AND SPEAK

What should you do if you find one of these items on the street or in a public place?

1.

2.

Jacket on the chair

3.

4.

What if find this

5.

6.

VOCABULARY EXPANSION 1

The prefixes **pre-/post** and **bi-/semi-**

Notice the meaning and formation of these words.
I saw that film before it opened. I saw a **preview** of it.
Prices were low before the war. **Prewar** prices were low.
Life after the war was hard. **Postwar** life was hard.
I put off the party for a week. I **postponed** the party.

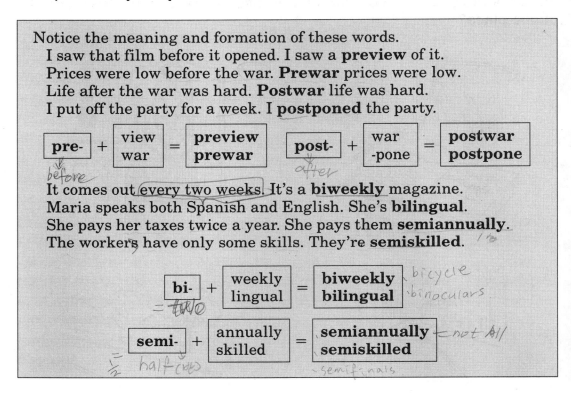

It comes out every two weeks. It's a **biweekly** magazine.
Maria speaks both Spanish and English. She's **bilingual**.
She pays her taxes twice a year. She pays them **semiannually**.
The workers have only some skills. They're **semiskilled**.

PRACTICE

Fill in the blanks with words from the following list.

biweekly   postwar   postpone   prewar   prepay   semiannually

1. Never _____ until tomorrow things you can do today.
2. Jan sees the dentist every six months. She sees him _____ .
3. She has to pay the dentist's fee <u>before</u> the appointment—she has to _____ the fee.
4. I make a loan payment every two weeks. I make _____ payments.
5. After the war, employment was high. _____ employment was high.
6. They gave the prize twice a year. They give the prize _____ .
7. That building was built before the war. It was a _____ building.

VOCABULARY EXPANSION 2

The prefixes **in-/im-/il-/ir-**

Notice the meaning and formation of these words.

You can't see odors. They're **invisible**. (not visible)
You can't travel to the sun. It's **impossible**. (not possible)
You can't smoke in the subway. It's **illegal**. (not legal)
You can't replace coal that is mined. It's **irreplaceable**. (not replaceable)

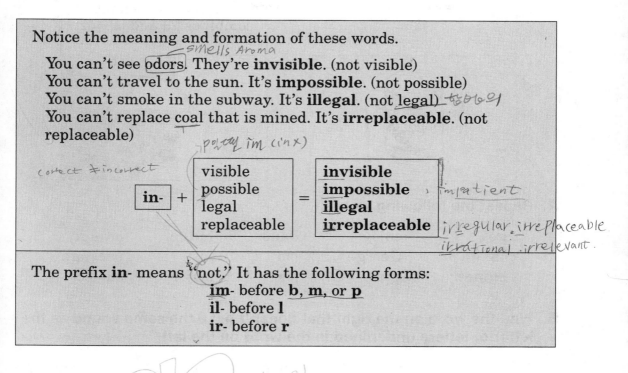

in- +	visible possible legal replaceable	=	**invisible** **impossible** **illegal** **irreplaceable**

The prefix **in-** means "not." It has the following forms:

im- before **b, m,** or **p**
il- before **l**
ir- before **r**

PRACTICE

Fill in the blanks with the correct form of the prefix in-.

1. That answer is wrong; it is ___correct.
2. Smoking may do ___reversible damage to your lungs.
3. Something that doesn't make sense is ___logical.
4. Hiring a member of your family can be ___proper.
5. Mt. Fuji is an ___active volcano.
6. The judge said that the evidence was ___relevant.
7. Sending an innocent person to prison is an ___justice.
8. We will all die someday; that is ___evitable.

PRONOUNCE: [ĭ]

jam	complex consonant combines [d] and [ž]: [dž]
	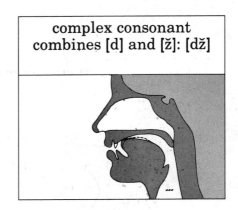

A. Repeat the following words.

ages	enjoy	Jane	judge	orange
change	George	job	just	package
engineer	gym	joke	major	subject

B. Find the word on the right that doesn't have the same sound as the letter or letters underlined in the word on the left.

1.	gem	general	orange	get	energy
2.	change	dangerous	against	intelligence	biology
3.	age	Jonathan	knowledge	urge	finger
4.	judo	girl	germs	gym	jacket
5.	gentle	injure	Virginia	give	subjects

C. Listen to this saying and repeat it.

We should have a general knowledge of the best foods to eat. We should encourage people of all ages to eat more fruits and vegetables. What are the major fruits and vegetables of your geographic region?

D. Listen to this saying and repeat it.

The end does not justify the means.

CONVERSATION

Solving a Crime

(handwritten notes: murder, theft, drug trafficing, terrorism, assault)

Tom Price and Linda Grant stopped at a drugstore, and Tom went inside to buy a newspaper. While Linda was waiting, she heard gunshots. She ran to a phone and called the police. When the police arrived, Tom was in the store, standing next to a dead body and holding a gun. A police officer has arrested Tom and a detective is questioning Linda.

DETECTIVE: Exactly what happened, Miss Grant?

LINDA: My friend Tom and I stopped here on our way to the movies, and he went inside to buy a newspaper. While I was waiting in the car, I heard shots, so I called the police.

DETECTIVE: Did you see anyone enter or leave the store?

LINDA: No, I didn't, ma'am.

35

OFFICER: I've informed Mr. Price of his rights, and he's decided to talk to us. He doesn't think he needs a lawyer.

DETECTIVE: O.K., Mr. Price. Can you tell me what happened?

TOM: I was walking toward the store when I heard shots. I pulled out my gun and went in very quietly. I saw a man leave by the back door. The cash register was empty, and the clerk was lying behind the counter.

OFFICER: It's a little dangerous to enter a place after you hear shots. Why did you go in?

TOM: It's hard to explain. I thought maybe I could help.

DETECTIVE: It's also very dangerous to carry a gun. Do you have a permit?

TOM: Yes, ma'am, I do. It's necessary for me to carry a gun because I work alone in a store very late at night.

OFFICER: Well, I'm going to have to take you to the station while the detectives study the scene of the crime.

LINDA: But I'm sure Tom is telling the truth. He's always honest.

DETECTIVE: I know both of you are upset. But we have to collect the

evidence. Then figuring out the truth won't be difficult.

Answer and Discuss

1. What happened after Tom and Linda stopped at the drugstore?
2. What did Linda do when she heard the shots?
3. Did Linda see anyone enter or leave the store?
4. According to U.S. law, Tom has the right to remain silent and have an attorney. What did Tom decide to do? Was this the right decision?
5. What is Tom's story?
6. Was it dangerous for Tom to enter the store? Why did he do it?
7. Is it good for a person like Tom to carry a gun? Why or why not?
8. According to the detective, figuring out the truth won't be difficult. What evidence would prove that Tom didn't kill the drugstore clerk?

INTERACTION

A. Play one of the two roles with a partner.

1. You are a police officer. Someone has stolen a television from a house, and you have come to make a report on the burglary. Ask the victim questions to find out as much as possible about the burglary.
2. You arrived home to find a burglar leaving with your television. Explain the details of the burglary to a police officer.

B. Play one of the two roles with a partner.

1. You are a police officer making a report on a street robbery. Ask the victim questions and write down all the details of the crime.
2. Someone stole your wallet or purse on the street. Describe exactly what happened to the police officer.

[handwritten: "to" has no meaning ⇒ not preposition / Able to work / Noun / adverb / Adjective / ex) Noun = To go seemed impossible / Adj : that's the place to go]

STUDY 1

It in the subject position for a delayed **to** infinitive:
It's dangerous to carry a gun.

[handwritten: Ad: we were waiting to go]

Notice the use of **it** in the subject position.

| **To leave now** | would be impolite. |

| **It** | would be impolite | **to leave now**. |

It's important **to be on time**.

It's dangerous **to drive in bad weather**.

Use **it** to fill the subject position when the **to** infinitive, the <u>real</u> subject of the sentence, <u>appears</u> later in the sentence.

PRACTICE

[handwritten: boring / adjective]

A. Combine the sentences using *it* in the subject position followed by a *to* infinitive.

[handwritten margin list: want, need, would, hope, expect, plan, intend, mean, decide, promise, offer, agree, refuse, seem, appear, pretend, forget, learn (know), try, can't afford to want]

EX. I like to go fishing. It's fun.
  ▷ **It's fun to go fishing.**

1. I have to find some bait. It's necessary.
  ▷ *It's necessary to find some bait.*

2. I hope I'll have some good weather, too. It's helpful.
  ▷ *It's helpful to have some good weather too*

3. I know how to use a fishing rod. It's easy.
▷ *It's easy to use a fishing rod*

4. You have to bait the hook carefully. It's important.
▷

5. You have to hold on to the rod tightly when fishing. It's difficult.
▷

6. I always try to catch a big fish. It's exciting.
▷

7. I don't like to catch little fish. It's disappointing.
▷

8. I know how to clean fish correctly. It's hard.
▷

9. I always cook fish over an open fire. It's fantastic.
▷ *It's fantastic [to] cook fish over an open fire*

10. I love to eat fresh fish. It's a pleasure.
▷ *It's a pleasure to eat fresh fish*

B. Change each sentence to an affirmative yes-no question using the cue. Then answer the question, giving your own opinion.

EX. It's fun to go fishing. (swimming)
▷ **Is it fun to go swimming? Yes, it is./No, it isn't.**

Does not need to in front

feel
hear
help } *emotional verb*
let
make
see
watch

1. It's dangerous to swim alone in a river. (the ocean)
▷ *Is it dangerous to swim alone in the ocean? Yes it is.*

2. It's expensive to go skiing. (for a walk)
▷

ex)
Bob felt the hot water on his body.
I heard the bell ring.

3. It's enjoyable to take a walk in the country. (city)
▷

4. It's exciting to go to a soccer match. (museum)
▷ *Is it exciting to go to a museum?*

5. It's important to work hard. (relax)
▷ *Is it important to relax?*

(handwritten at top: It is (+) adjective (+) for (+) infinitive phrase — 3개의 늘이 꼭 들어있다. to infinitive 예문)

(handwritten: You should stud hard — noun — It is important for you to study hard. It's important. You to learn to drive)

40

(handwritten: It's hard for me to go to sleep)

STUDY 2

It in the subject position for a delayed **to** infinitive introduced by a **for** phrase: *It's necessary for me to carry a gun.*

Notice the position and use of the **for** phrase and the **to** infinitive.

(handwritten: for 발음 always 약하게 (pronouce 시 약하게된다))

It	wasn't easy	**for Tom to prove his story was true.**
It	isn't difficult	**for the detective to figure out the truth.**

Use the **for** phrase with the **to** infinitive after certain adjectives or nouns when the subject of the infinitive is important to the meaning of the sentence.

PRACTICE

Using the two sentences given, form a new sentence beginning with *it*. The sentence should contain a phrase with *for*.

EX. A runner must practice every day.
     It's important.
   ▷ **It's important for a runner to practice every day.**

1. A runner has to keep in shape.
    It's necessary.
   ▷ *It's necessary for a runner to keep in shape.*

2. A runner should eat well.
    It's essential.
   ▷ *It's essential for a runner to eat well.*

3. A runner needs to get enough rest.
    It's advisable.
   ▷ *It's advisable for a runner to get enough rest.*

4. A runner should compete with others.
    It's useful.
   ▷ *It's useful for a runner to compete with others.*

B) We don't have to go to the meeting
→ It isn't necessary for us to go to the meeting.

C) A dog can't talk.
→ It's impossible for a dog to talk.

hw

STUDY 3

The -ing form of the verb as subject:
Figuring out the truth won't be difficult.

gerund
-ing studying

Notice the use and position of the -ing form of the verb.

의미는 같다.

It's important	**to eat.**		**Eating** is important.
It's necessary	**to study.**		**Studying** is necessary.
It isn't good	**to be late.**		**Being late** isn't good.

-ing form이 앞에 나오면 subj 이다.

You can use the **-ing form** of the **verb** as the subject of a sentence.

PRACTICE

Make sentences like the model. Use the *-ing* form as the subject.

EX. It takes experience to plan a good meal.
▷ **Planning a good meal takes experience.**

-은 대지 않지 마라.

1. It's a good idea to serve vegetables, a starch, and meat or fish.
▷

using verb as a subject

2. It's important to cook meat well.
▷

It's important to study
⇒ studying is important.

3. It's easy to boil potatoes.
▷

4. It takes patience to cut up vegetables.
▷ cuting up vegetables takes patience.

5. It can be fun to prepare a good meal.
▷   ing   can be fun

42

STUDY 4

Quantifiers as noun substitutes: *I know both of you are upset.*

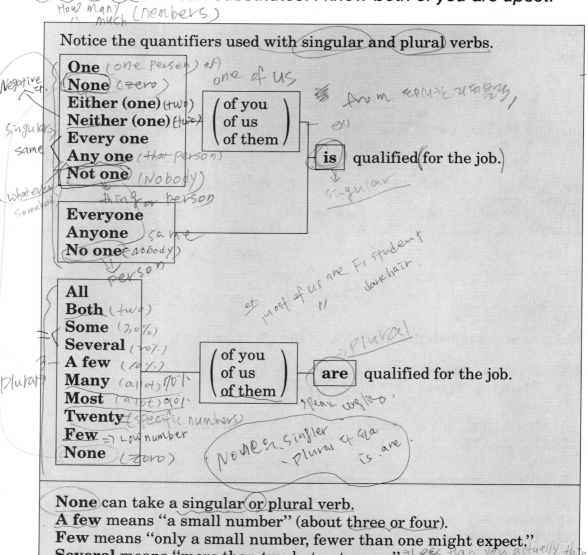

Notice the quantifiers used with **singular** and **plural** verbs.

One		
None		
Either (one)		
Neither (one)	(of you / of us / of them)	**is** qualified for the job.
Every one		
Any one		
Not one		

Everyone	
Anyone	
No one	

All		
Both		
Some		
Several		
A few	(of you / of us / of them)	**are** qualified for the job.
Many		
Most		
Twenty		
Few		
None		

None can take a singular or plural verb.
A few means "a small number" (about three or four).
Few means "only a small number, fewer than one might expect."
Several means "more than two but not many."

The modifying phrase beginning with **of** may sometimes be omitted when the context or situation is already known.
Everyone, anyone, and **no one** are not followed by **of.**

PRACTICE

Fill in the appropriate quantifier from the following list. Each quantifier is used once.

all	everyone	four	neither	several
both (two people)	few	most	no one (zero)	some

EX. The whole company wants to have an office party.   *lik*
   _____**All**_____ of the employees want to have an office party.

1. Pablo and Lin want to plan the party.
   _____Both_____ of them want to plan the party.

2. Two or three of the employees plan to bring tapes.
   _____Several_____ of the employees plan to bring tapes.

3. Almost all of the employees dance well.
   _____Most_____ of the employees dance well.

4. Helen, Ana, Ben, and Raul are excellent dancers.
   _____four_____ of the employees are excellent dancers.

5. All of the employees are going to eat a lot of food.
   _____Everyone_____ is going to eat a lot of food.

6. There isn't one employee who wants to miss the party.
   _____No one_____ wants to miss it.

7. But Igor and Estela <u>can't</u> come to the party.
   _____Neither_____ of them can come.

8. <u>Not many</u> of the employees will leave the party early.
   _____few_____
   _____some_____ of the employees will leave early.

9. <u>Not everyone</u> will stay until the end of the party.
   _____Some_____ of the employees probably won't stay to clean up.

LISTEN

A. Listen carefully to the information. Then choose the statement that is true according to the information you have heard.

1. a. They're not going on vacation this year.
   b. They're going on vacation in July.
   c. They're going on vacation in December.

2. a. We don't like each other.
   b. We agree on everything.
   c. We like each other.

3. a. Someone stole a car.
   b. Someone stole her luggage.
   c. Someone lost her luggage.

4. a. Many of the employees attended the meeting.
   b. Mrs. Rivera didn't hold the meeting.
   c. Mrs. Rivera held the meeting.

   dozen = 12개

5. a. Twelve were unbroken. = not broken
   b. Nine were unbroken.
   c. Three were unbroken.

6. a. Exercise is always good.
   b. Too much exercise is bad.
   c. Exercise is never good.

B. Listen carefully to the information. Then choose the correct answer.

1. a. The library.
   b. Magazines and newspapers.
   c. The encyclopedias. (Book of information

2. a. A doctor.
   b. A teacher.
   c. A student.

3. a. The passenger smokes.
   b. There is no smoking.
   c. Smoking is not allowed.

   I can't smoke

4. a. In a library.
   b. In a college bookstore.
   c. In a grocery store.

READ

How to Make Friends

be frendly

"No man is an island" is a well-known line from John Donne's *Devotions Upon Emergent Occasions,* written more than 300 years ago. His meaning then is still true today. No one can live a completely isolated life. Without other people, life becomes empty and sad. We all need to have friends.

However, for some of us, making friends is not easy. Feeling shy, we may hesitate to make the first move. It is also difficult at times to keep the friends we already have. Many people ask themselves, "What am I doing wrong? How can I make more people like me?"

There are many books about friendship, but Dale Carnegie's *How to Win Friends and Influence People,* written in 1936, is the most famous. A "how to" book about dealing with other people, it became an instant best-seller. It was later translated into twenty-eight languages.

Although Carnegie's suggestions seem to be simple at first, it really takes some effort to apply them. Can his advice help you in your contact with people? Do you need to change the way you act? Examine the following list of suggestions from Carnegie's book.

1. *Be friendly and courteous.* Always greet people with a smile. The next time you see someone without a smile, give that person one of yours. Be polite. Begin your requests with little phrases like, "I'm sorry to bother you," "Would you please," "Would you mind," or "Excuse me." Remember to say "Thank you." Finally, answer all questions in a friendly manner, and be as helpful as you can.

2. *Go out of your way to be nice.* Find some time to do special things for other people. Making an extra cup of soup for a sick neighbor may seem like a little thing to you, but it will make your neighbor feel a lot better.

3. *Remember names.* Concentrate hard when you are introduced to someone, and remember the person's name. They say that the sweetest music to a person's ears is the sound of his or her own name.

4. *Be tolerant.* Try to understand other people's ways and, in so doing, learn something from them.

5. *Listen patiently.* Don't constantly interrupt or contradict other people. Learn to listen carefully. Encourage people to tell you about their accomplishments, and praise them for their achievements.

   Dale Carnegie wrote his book because he found that most people need to get along with others. He also knew that most people are interested in learning how to make friends.

Answer and Discuss

1. Who wrote, "No man is an island..."? Do you agree with the quotation? Give reasons.
2. Is it easy for everyone to make friends? Explain your answer.
3. Who wrote *How to Win Friends and Influence People?*
4. How do you know that the book was popular?
5. How should you greet people?
6. What are some polite phrases to use when making a request?
7. Is it important to remember people's names? Why?
8. What are some other rules for making friends?
9. Which of the rules of conduct do you need to work on the most?
10. Would you read Carnegie's book? Give reasons.

PHRASAL VERBS

Break into, get away, get away with, and **make up**

Notice the meaning of these phrasal verbs.

A man **broke into** the drugstore last night. Someone tried to stop him, but he **got away**. When he was arrested, he **made up** a good story. The police believed his story, and he **got away with** the crime.

Break into (nonseparable) means "enter forcibly."
Get away means "escape." It does not take a direct object.
Get away with (nonseparable) means "escape punishment for."
Make up (separable) means "invent."

PRACTICE

Complete the sentences using the correct form of a verb below.

break   get   get away with   make up
break into   get away   make

Susan lost the keys to her house one day. When she _____ home, no one was there. She realized that she had to _____ the house. She went to every window, but she couldn't open any of them. She finally decided to _____ a window and climb through it. Susan was tired and went upstairs to bed. Then her father and mother came home. Her father said, "Someone has _____ a window! A burglar has _____ the house!" Susan's mother and father searched the house and found no one. Her mother said, "The burglar has _____!" They called the police. The police said, "There have been many phone calls about a burglar—this person has _____ three burglaries just this week. Finally Susan woke up and came downstairs. "You're _____ a mistake," she said. "I _____ the house—there was no burglar." "I can't believe it," said her mother. "I hope you're not _____ this _____." "No, it's true," answered Susan. "I lost my keys, no one was home, and I _____ a bad decision. I'll pay for the broken window."

THINK AND SPEAK

Imagine that you are one of the people in on each of these pictures. What do you think you should do?

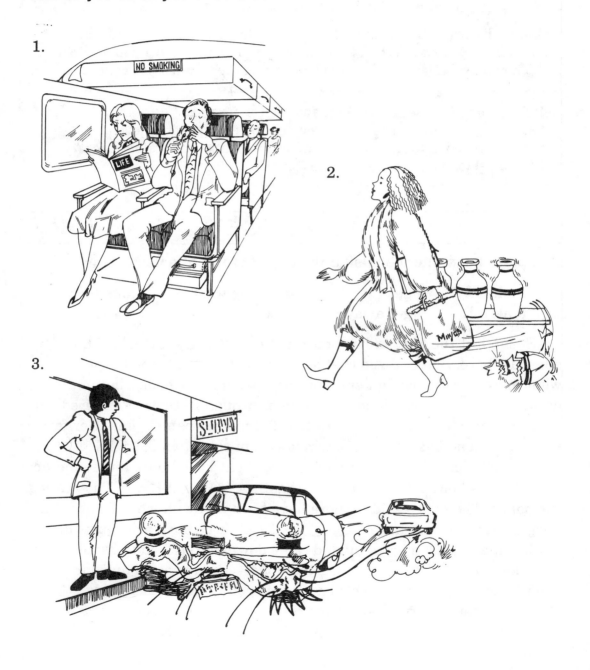

1.

2.

3.

VOCABULARY EXPANSION

The prefixes **un-**, **dis-**, and **en-**

Notice the meaning and formation of these words.

I wasn't able to finish my work. I was **unable** to finish it.
That politician isn't popular. He's **unpopular**.
Jane isn't employed right now. She's **unemployed** right now.
Some laws aren't fair. Some laws are **unfair**.

The car accident left him unable to walk. It **disabled** him.
My wallet was here, and now it's gone. It has **disappeared**.
George isn't honest. He's **dishonest**.
Kim's letter didn't please me. It **displeased** me.

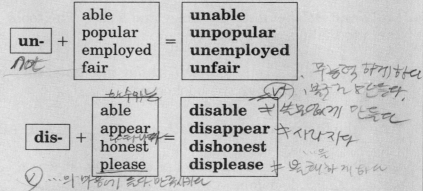

un- +	able popular employed fair	=	**unable** **unpopular** **unemployed** **unfair**
dis- +	able appear honest please	=	**disable** **disappear** **dishonest** **displease**

I'm going to make the kitchen larger. I'm going to **enlarge** it.
You gave me some money. It **enabled** me to pay my bills.
They gave me the authority to make financial decisions.
They **empowered** me to make financial decisions.

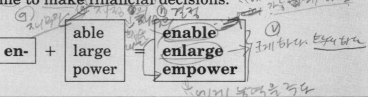

en- +	able large power	=	**enable** **enlarge** **empower**

The prefix **un-** means "not."
The prefix **dis-** means "not" or "opposite of."
The prefix **en-** means "to make (adjective)" or "to give (noun) to."
En- before p or b becomes **em-**.

PRACTICE

A. Complete each sentence using the correct form of one of the words below.

disagree	dishonest	enable	unemployed
disappear	displeased	unable	unpopular

1. Where's my purse? It just _disappeared_.

2. Our teacher is _displeased_ because we didn't do our homework assignment correctly.

3. Tom and Linda are never _dishonest_. They always tell the truth.

4. Sally and Bob bought a hammer and a saw. The tools _enabled_ them to make some bookcases.

5. They also bought some nails. Without the nails, they would have been _unable_ to make the bookcases.

6. After the factory closed, my father was _unemployed_ for six months.

7. The city council voted to increase our taxes. It was a very _unpopular_ decision.

8. I'm a Democrat, and my friend is a Republican. When we discuss politics, we usually _disagree_.

0

0

0

B. Complete the sentences by using the prefixes un-, dis-, and en-.

1. Some people think that water is *un* important.
2. Life without water would have many *dis* advantages.
3. Without lakes or oceans, our vacations would be *un* interesting.
4. Without water, everything would be *un* clean.
5. It would be *dis* tasteful to eat from *un* washed dishes.
6. Water *un*ables people to live.
7. It dissolves the nutrients in soil and ___ables plants to absorb them.
8. Without water, farmers would soon be *un* employed.
9. In fact, without water, all life would *dis* appear.
10. That is why the government ___courages people to use less water and ___courages them from wasting water.

(+) en courage someone / to do / something
(−) dis courage someone / from doing / something

PRONOUNCE: [y]

yam	consonant glide, tongue very high in center-front position
	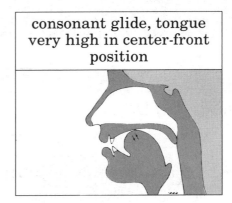

A. Repeat the following words.

popular	onion	useful	yet
canyon	United States	usually	you
million	university	year	young

B. On a sheet of paper, write the numbers of words that have the sound [y] as in yam.

1. yes	6. onion	11. true
2. amuse	7. youth	12. view
3. usual	8. Lynn	13. unique
4. university	9. canyon	14. uncle
5. unable	10. Daniel	15. beautiful

C. Listen to this saying and repeat it.

A university education is very important in today's world. In the United States, there are millions of people studying in universities. They want to learn useful skills so that they can get good jobs and have secure futures. It usually takes four years to get a university degree.

D. Listen to this saying and repeat it.

A snow **year**, a rich **year**.

CONVERSATION

An Emergency Decision

Julia and Max are fishing together on a river. Suddenly they hear someone calling for help. It's a little boy who is drowning. They have to decide what to do immediately.

VOICE: Help!

MAX: I hear someone screaming. Do you hear anything?

JULIA: Yes. Someone's calling out for help. Look! He's drowning!

MAX: What can we do? I can swim, but I can't rescue anyone.

JULIA: I'm not a good swimmer, but I'm going in anyway.

53

54

MAX: Wait, Julia. That's very dangerous. He could pull you under, and the water is very deep.

JULIA: But we can't let him drown.

MAX: I know! Remember our swimming class? They taught us other ways to rescue people.

JULIA: You're right! They advised us to extend something to the person, like a rope or a branch.

MAX: Look! Here's a long branch. Help me carry it.

(Max and Julia carry the branch to the water. Together, they extend it toward the little boy.)

JULIA: *(To the boy.)* Grab this branch and hang onto it!

MAX: We're in luck. The current is pulling him in our direction.

(The boy grabs onto the branch, and Max and Julia pull him to the edge of the river. They pull him out and carry him to a blanket.)

JULIA: *(To the boy.)* Are you O.K.? Put this blanket around you.

MAX: Just relax now. Everything is going to be all right.

Answer and Discuss

1. What did Max and Julia hear? *here bin //*
2. What is happening in the river?
3. What does Julia <u>want to do</u>?
4. Why doesn't Max want her to go into the river? *(He could pull under*
5. What does Max remember finally?
6. What do Max and Julia decide to do?
7. What does Julia tell the little boy to do? *Grab this branch and hang onto it!*
8. How do Max and Julia get the little boy out of the water? *put the blanket arunt him*
9. What do Max and Julia tell the boy to do after they pull him out of the water?
10. What advice should they give the little boy?

INTERACTION

Look at the picture of the car accident. Then, with a partner, play one of the roles listed.

future

1. The traffic light was green. You were trying to make a left turn. (People drive on the right side of the road in this country.) You thought the lane you were crossing was clear, but a car hit you on the passenger side door. You are not hurt, but you are angry.
2. You were traveling at a normal speed when suddenly a car making a left turn crossed your lane. You could not stop in time and hit the car. You just want to get the other driver's name and address and insurance information because you are late for an appointment.

STUDY 1

The infinitive as the object of a verb: *We can't let him drown.*

Notice the use of the infinitive without **to** and with its subject.

Max and Julia | **heard** | the boy.
The boy | **screamed.**

Max and Julia | **heard** | **the boy** | **scream.**

SUBJECT OF SENTENCE	VERB	SUBJECT OF INFINITIVE	INFINITIVE	
They	**saw**	**him**	**go**	down.
They	**watched**	**him**	**struggle.**	
They	**didn't let**	**the boy**	**drown.**	
Julia	**helped**	**Max**	**carry**	the branch.
Julia	**made**	**Max**	**put**	the blanket around him.

The subject of the infinitive is expressed when it is different from that of the verb. Use the object form of the pronoun for the subject of the infinitive.

(handwritten annotations at top of page)

※ Subject(t) verb(t) object(t) Infinitive ≫ ※ infinitive
formular form

ex) They made Sally open her suitcase

PRACTICE

Hot weather makes me feel tired.

≪ Adjectives followed by infinitive ≫ infinitive
to see Bob.

describe Noun   Adjective
show
color   ex) I was surprised
shape
size
feeling

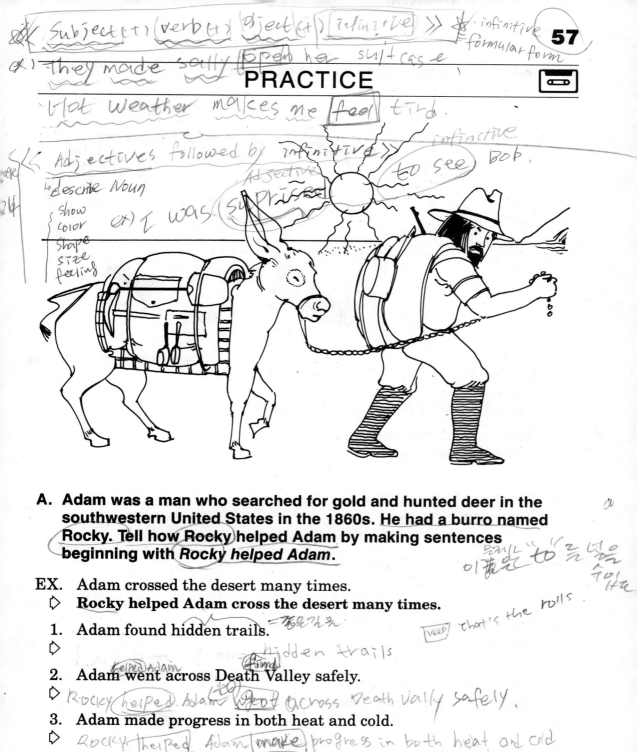

A. **Adam was a man who searched for gold and hunted deer in the southwestern United States in the 1860s. He had a burro named Rocky. Tell how Rocky helped Adam by making sentences beginning with *Rocky helped Adam*.**

EX.   Adam crossed the desert many times.
▷ **Rocky helped Adam cross the desert many times.**

1. Adam found hidden trails.
▷   hidden trails

2. Adam went across Death Valley safely.
▷ Rocky helped Adam went across Death Vally safely.

3. Adam made progress in both heat and cold.
▷ Rocky helped Adam make progress in both heat and cold

4. Adam carried heavy bundles up the mountains.
▷
     Rocky helped Adam carry heavy bundles up the mountains.

B. Combine these sentences as in the example.

EX. Rocky followed Adam through the snow.
Adam let him.
▷ **Adam let Rocky follow him through the snow.**

1. Rocky ate grass under the snow.
Adam watched him.
▷

2. Rocky fell through the snow once.
Adam saw him.
▷

3. Rocky climbed out of the snow.
Adam helped him.
▷

4. Rocky lay on a blanket to rest.
Adam made him.
▷

5. Some animals made noise.
Adam and Rocky heard them.
▷

6. Some deer ran past Adam and Rocky.
Adam and Rocky saw them.
▷

A &R saw   s noedeer

STUDY 2

The use of the **to** infinitive after certain verbs:
They advised us to extend something to the person.

subject + verb + object + infinitive

Notice the use of the **to** infinitive with these three groups of verbs.

1. With the subject omitted:

Sub + verb + infinitive (No Object)

| David | tried
learned
hoped
planned
intended
forgot | to play | the piano. |

2. With the subject expressed:

subject + verb + (object) + infinitive .

| His parents | told
advised
permitted
forced | him | to take | piano lessons. |

3. With or without an expressed subject:

| I | wanted
asked
expected | (him) | to drive | the car. |

The verbs in these three groups are followed by a **to** infinitive.
The subject of each verb in group 1 is the same as the subject of the
  infinitive. Thus, the subject of the infinitive is omitted.
The subject of each verb in group 2 is different from the subject of
  the infinitive. Thus, the subject of the infinitive must be given.
In group 3, when the subject of the verb is the same as the subject of
  the infinitive, the subject of the infinitive is not given. When it is
  different, the subject of the infinitive must be given.

PRACTICE

A. Jack is a stranger who joins Adam in the mountains. Expand the second sentence in each pair as in the example.

EX. Adam needed to leave the mountains soon.
     Jack advised Adam to.
  ▷ **Jack advised Adam to leave the mountains soon.**

1. Adam was going to leave the mountains soon.
    Adam decided to.
  ▷ *Adam decided to leave the mountains soon.*

2. Adam was going to take Rocky with him.
    Adam decided to.
  ▷ *Adam decided to take Rocky with him.*

3. Jack was going to go down the mountain
    with Adam.
    Adam asked Jack to.
  ▷ *Adam asked Jack to go down the mountain
    with Adam.*

4. Adam packed up his things.
    Jack urged Adam to.
  ▷ *Jack urged Adam to packed up
    his things.*

5. Adam shared his food with Jack.
    Adam agreed to.
  ▷ *Adam agreed to shared his food with Jack*

6. Jack prepared bread and beans.
    Adam asked Jack to.
  ▷ *Adam asked Jack to prepared bread and beans.*

7. Adam and Jack changed their minds.
    A storm forced Adam and Jack to.
  ▷

B. Expand the second sentence in each pair.

EX.   I took piano lessons.
      My mother forced me to.
▷   **My mother forced me to take piano lessons.**

1.   I learned to play the piano.
     I didn't want to.
▷

2.   I practiced regularly.
     My piano teacher expected me to. practice regulary
▷

3.   I practiced an hour a day.
     She told me to. Plactice an hour a day.
▷

4.   My mother helped me.
     I asked my mother to. help me
▷

5.   I wanted to play well.
     I really tried to. pluy well
▷

6.   I tried to please my mother.
     I wanted to. Please my mother
▷

7.   I planned to continue my piano lessons.
     My teacher advised me to.
▷

8.   My mother thought I could play in a concert hall someday.
     My mother wanted me to. Play in a Concert hall someday
▷

9.   But I stopped taking piano lessons.
     My mother permitted me to. Stop taking piano lessons.
▷

LISTEN

A. Listen carefully to the information. Then choose the statement that is true according to the information you have heard.

1. a. Olga spent $60.
    b. Olga spent $40.
    c. Olga spent $20.

2. a. Kim is older and taller.
    b. Kim's sister is older and taller.
    c. Kim's sister is younger but taller.

3. a. His plane left at noon.
    b. His plane left at 11:30.
    c. His plane left at 12:30.

4. a. Gary's class is tomorrow.
    b. Gary's class is tonight.
    c. Gary's class is today.

5. a. It's not convenient to have the meeting.
    b. The time should be convenient for everyone.
    c. The plan is not convenient for everyone.

6. a. The bill was $30.
    b. The bill was $7.50.
    c. The bill was $15.

B. Listen carefully to the information. Then choose the correct answer.

1. a. Miss Lopez.
    b. Alice Sullivan.
    c. Miss Lopez's assistant.

2. a. Jaggar.
    b. Jaegger.
    c. Jagger.

3. a. Go camping.
    b. Go skiing.
    c. Go fishing.

4. a. Boss and assistant.
    b. Cashier and customer.
    c. Clerk and customer.

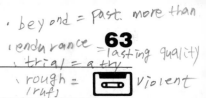

READ

Marathon Woman

A heart disease at the age of sixteen stopped Diana Nyad from competing in the 1968 Olympics, but it didn't stop her from pushing herself almost beyond endurance in marathon swimming. Her courage took her from trial to trial, leading to a heroic effort on August 13, 1978. On that day, she tried to swim farther than anyone had ever swum in the open sea. Why, at the age of twenty-eight, did Diana Nyad plan to swim 103 miles, from Ortegaso Beach, Cuba, to Key West, Florida? Nyad's answer to that question was, "This is my Olympics."

Diana Nyad had already proven her ability. She began swimming in the seventh grade and became a state swimming champion that same year. Over the next five years, she set many new world records.

Nyad had the perfect body for a swimmer, with great strength in her upper body and very little weight in her hips and legs. For the 103-mile swim, her daily training routine included the following: 10 miles of running in 62 minutes; 2 hours of fast pool swimming: half an hour of rope skipping; food totaling 5,000 calories. Twice a week, she worked out on swimmers' weight machines.

Some days Nyad did more of one exercise and less of another. But by the tenth month, she was swimming 7 hours a day and about 24 hours each weekend. She was eating 12,000 calories every day. Just before the big swim, she stopped all physical training. She just slept and ate in order to gain 20 pounds, the amount she would lose during the swim.

Nyad's training was hard financially as well as physically. In order to hire trainers and buy "Cleopatra," a $42,000 cage to protect her from sharks, she had to find sponsors to pay expenses of more than $150,000.

One Sunday, August 13, Nyad began the long swim. From the beginning, the rough sea made her progress difficult. She bounced back and forth against the walls of the cage. During one 6-hour period, she actually lost 2 miles instead of progressing. Strong winds forced Cleopatra farther and farther off the course. Finally, after 41 hours and 70 miles, Nyad's trainers saw that she could not reach Key West. Because there was no other land nearby, they had to take her in a boat. "I quit," she said. "I've never done anything so hard in my life."

In August 1979, Nyad made two attempts to swim from North Bimini Island in the Bahamas to Florida. The first time, she had to quit after 12½ hours when she was stung and partially paralyzed by a Portuguese man-of-war, a blue sea creature with long, stinging tentacles attached to a floating sac. The second time, she struggled for 27½ hours against the powerful Gulf Stream and swam ashore at Juno Beach, Florida, to the cheers and hugs of waiting spectators. Her left eye was swollen shut from salt water and her body tortured by stings, blisters, and swellings. She had also endured seasickness, fatigue, and hallucinations while swimming a distance of 89 miles.

Answer and Discuss

1. Why didn't Diana Nyad compete in the 1968 Olympics?
2. What did she prepare to do in 1978?
3. What was her training routine?
4. Why did she need to gain weight before the marathon swim?
5. What training expenses did Nyad have? How did she meet them?
6. Why did she have trouble from the beginning of the swim?
7. What effect did the strong winds have on her progress?
8. How long did Nyad swim before she had to stop?
9. Where did she begin her two swims in August 1979?
10. Why did she have to stop the first of these swims?
11. Besides the torture to her body, what else did Nyad endure during her swim to Juno Beach?

PHRASAL VERBS

Call out, look out (for), and **take off**

Notice the meaning of these phrasal verbs.

Julia and Max heard a little boy **call out to** them.
He was drowning and was **calling out for** help.
His mother had told him to **look out for** strong currents.
Julia was ready to **take** her shoes **off** and jump in the water.
But Max stopped her. He was **looking out for** her safety.

Call out (nonseparable) means "shout" (something). It can also be followed by **to** and **for.**
Look out (for) means "be alert" (to danger). By itself, **look out** does not take a direct object. Followed by **for,** it takes a direct object and is nonseparable.

PRACTICE

Complete the sentences using the correct form of an appropriate verb from the following list.

| call | look at | look out for | take off |
| call out | look out | take | look for |

1. Alice and I _____**took**_____ a long hike in the mountains in order to ___**look for**___ fossils.
2. The guide told us to __**look out for**__ poisonous snakes.
3. She told us that we shouldn't ___**take off**___ our boots.
4. Suddenly I realized that Alice was missing, and I began to ___**call out**___ her name.
5. I continued to ____**call**____ her for a long time.
6. When I found her, she was ___**looking at**___ something on the ground.
7. It was a poisonous snake. "___**Look out!**___!" she said.
8. I'm waiting for it to leave so that I can ___**take**___ the fossil lying next to it."

THINK AND SPEAK

How did the people in these pictures get into these situations? Tell what you think is going to happen to each person. Give a safety rule to follow in each situation. You may want to use the words given.

1.

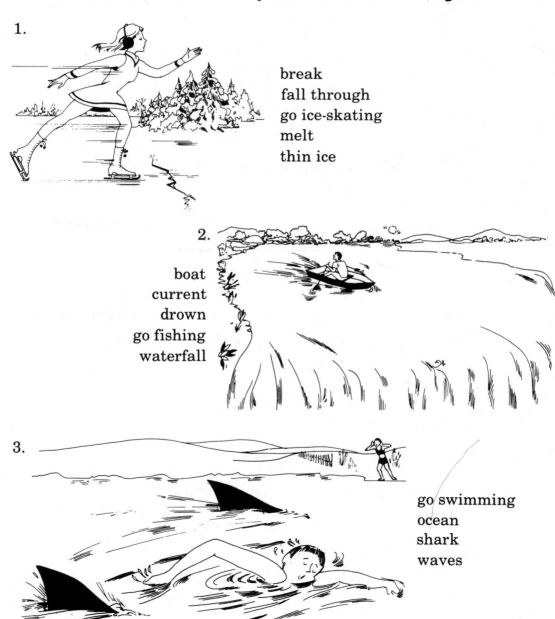

break
fall through
go ice-skating
melt
thin ice

2.

boat
current
drown
go fishing
waterfall

3.

go swimming
ocean
shark
waves

VOCABULARY EXPANSION

The prefixes inter-, intra-, extra-, trans-, and tele-

Notice the meaning and formation of these words.

Trade between nations is **international** trade.
Travel between planets is **interplanetary** travel.
The university soccer teams that play each other are part of an
  intramural sports program.
Feeding a patient by putting a solution directly into a vein is
  intravenous feeding.

inter-	+	national planetary	=	**international** **interplanetary**

interpose = go between
intercomunicate
interfere communicate
interdependence each other
interchangeable

intra-	+	mural venous	=	**intramural** **intravenous**

= inside
intravert.

School activities held after class are **extracurricular** activities.
The movie was out of the ordinary. It was **extraordinary**.

=	extra-	+	curricular ordinary	=	**extracurricular** **extraordinary**

more
extravagant

They made the factory into apartments. They **transformed** it.
They planted the tree in another place. They **transplanted** it.
I talk to my mother on the **telephone** every day.
I can't go to the game, but I'll watch it on **television**.

trans-	+	form plant	=	**transform** **transplant**

→across
transmission =across diseases
transport

tele-	+	phone vision	=	**telephone** **television**

distant
telecast
telescope

The prefix **inter-** means "between."
The prefix **intra-** means "within, inside."
The prefix **extra-** means "outside, besides, more than."
The prefix **trans-** means "across, beyond."
The prefix **tele-** means "distant, at a distance."

PRACTICE

A. Complete each sentence using the correct form of one of these words.

extracurricular	international	transform
extraordinary	interview	translate
extravagant	telephone	transplant
intravenous		

1. Can you _____ this letter into English for me?

2. Do you take part in any _____ activities at school?

3. Did your job _____ go well?

4. Can you order things by _____ from that store?

5. They spend a lot of money on their clothes. They're _____.

6. It's hard to believe that I ran into you like this. It's an _____ coincidence.

7. The United Nations devotes itself to _____ problems.

8. The patient needed a new heart, so the doctors performed a heart _____ operation.

9. The nurse attached some tubes to his arm and fed him _____.

10. The operation completely _____ the patient. He became stronger and more youthful than he was before.

B. Fill in the blanks with the prefixes *extra-*, *inter-*, *tele-*, and *trans-*.

A Century of Progress

During the twentieth century, we have seen _____ ordinary progress in the areas of _____ portation and communication. The use of the _____ phone for _____ national communication has grown tremendously. These days, _____ grams are almost obsolete. _____ continental and _____ continental travel are becoming possible for more and more people. And _inter_ planetary travel may become a possibility soon. Before this century, _____ scopes gave us our closest look at the moon. In this century, millions of people saw astronauts walk on the moon on _tele_ vision. While scientists talked to the astronauts, their conversation was _tele_ vised _inter_ nationally and _trans_ lated into many languages.

PRONOUNCE: [ǰ] and [y]

jam [ǰ]	yam [y]
	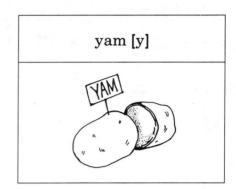

A. Repeat the following words.

agent	gentle	Nigeria	canyon	**university**	yes
average	jacket	oxygen	million	unusual	yet
cage	Japan	page	onion	use	you
change	jet	suggest	united	year	young

B. Listen to these words. On a sheet of paper, write *a* if you hear the sound [y] as in *yam*, *b* if you hear [ǰ] as in *jam*, and *c* if a word has neither sound.

1. year	5. use	9. Japan	13. under
2. gentle	6. go	10. general	14. college
3. leg	7. jewels	11. yellow	15. young
4. yet	8. William	12. George	16. regard

C. Listen to this saying and repeat it.

Millions of tourists visit many countries every year. Some enjoy seeing museums, monuments, and churches. Others prefer to relax on a warm beach or in a cool mountain area. What kind of tourist are you?

D. Listen to this saying and repeat it.

Jud**g**e not, that **y**ou be not **j**ud**g**ed.

CONVERSATION

Refusing an Invitation

내가너무 (1) 조심
네친구가

David and Ling are high school classmates. David wants to get to know Ling better, so he invites her to go to the movies with him.

DAVID: Would you like to go to the movies tonight?

LING: I'd like to, but I already have other plans.

DAVID: What about tomorrow night?

LING: Tomorrow night I'm going out with a group of friends. Why

don't you come with us?

How abot the days after tomorrow?
tomorrow 다음날.

DAVID: I was hoping that we could go out alone.

LING: Well, I really enjoy being with my friends. We always have a good time together, and Paul tells great jokes.

DAVID: I don't like going out in groups. I'd rather just talk to one person at a time.

LING: Well, I'm sure a lot of people would be delighted to go to a movie with you.

DAVID: Probably, but I'd rather go with you.

LING: I'm really sorry, but I can't... Listen, I have a class now.

DAVID: O.K. I'll see you later.

LING: Good-bye.

Answer and Discuss

1. What does David invite Ling to do tonight?
2. Why won't Ling go with him?
3. What is she going to do tomorrow night?
4. Why doesn't David want to go out with her group of friends?
5. Why does Ling want to go out in a group?
6. In your opinion, does David insist too much?
7. How do you think Ling feels about David?

8. Do you prefer to go out in a group or with just one other person?
9. What do students in your country do in a situation like Ling's?
10. Ling didn't tell David what her plans for tonight were. Do you think it's polite to refuse an invitation that way?

INTERACTION

A. Read the following invitation. Then, with a partner, play one of the roles described.

> *You are invited to* _____
> *For* _____
> *Given by* _____
> *On* _____
> *At* _____
> *645-1516 Regrets only*

1. You are giving the party, and you have sent written invitations. One of your friends calls to tell you that he or she cannot attend.
2. You have received an invitation to a party. You'd like to accept it, but you can't because you have already made plans for that evening. Call your friend and refuse the invitation politely. Tell your friend why you can't go.

B. Read the following situation. Then, with a partner, play one of the roles described.

There is a new Japanese movie in town that has won several prizes.

1. You want to see the movie, but you don't want to go alone. Call a friend and try to persuade him or her to go with you.
2. A friend invites you to go to a movie with him or her. Either accept or reject the invitation, but be as polite as possible.

ex) I'm [happy] to be here. (handwritten)

STUDY 1

Adjectives with the **to** infinitive:
A lot of people would be delighted to go to a movie with you.

Notice the position of the adjective and the **to** infinitive.

You're back from your trip. You seem happy.

You seem | **happy to be** | back from your trip.

You want to tell me about the trip. You look impatient.

You look | **impatient to tell** | me about the trip.

I want to have dinner with you tonight. I'd be delighted.

I'd be | **delighted to have** | dinner with you tonight.

You can use the **to** infinitive with adjectives that express emotional states—for example, **afraid, careful, certain, content, eager, fortunate, glad, happy, impatient, likely, lucky, pleased, proud, ready, sorry,** and **sure.**

These adjectives follow the verbs **appear, be, feel, look, seem,** and **sound.**

PRACTICE

Carlos's friend Lucy has moved to another town to take a job. She recently came back for a visit. Combine each pair of sentences as in the example.

EX.   Lucy was back in town.
      Lucy seemed happy.

▷ **Lucy seemed happy to be back in town.**

1.   Carlos ran into her.
     Carlos was delighted.

▷ *Carlos was delighted to run into her.* (handwritten)

2. Carlos and Lucy wanted to have dinner together at a restaurant.
Carlos and Lucy were eager.
▷ Carlos and Lucy ~~wanted to~~ *were* eager ~~to have~~ dinner ~~to eat~~ at a restaurant.

3. They saw an old friend there.
They were glad.
▷ They were glad to see an old friend there.

4. He joined them for dinner.
He seemed pleased.
▷ He seemed pleased to join them for dinner.

5. They wanted to try everything on the menu.
They were eager.
▷ They were eager ~~want~~ to try everything on the menu.

6. Carlos wanted to hear about Lucy's new job.
Carlos was impatient.
▷ Carlos was impatient ~~wanted~~ to hear about Lucy's new job.

7. Lucy wanted to talk about her job.
Lucy looked eager.
▷ Lucy looked eager ✓

8. She got a job as a sales representative for a computer company.
She felt lucky.
▷

9. She travels a lot.
She's fortunate.
▷

10. They left the restaurant and said good-bye.
They were sorry.
▷

76

(handwritten: « verb + infinitive or gerund » No difference in meaning
ex) It began to rain / It began raining.
· It started to work / It started working.
· They denied to steal the money / They denied stealing the money
avoid 동명사만)

STUDY 2

The -ing form of the verb as object:
I really enjoy being with my friends.

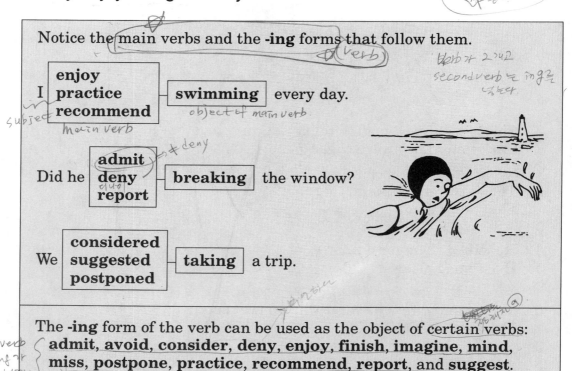

Notice the main verbs and the **-ing** forms that follow them.

I **enjoy / practice / recommend** — **swimming** every day.

Did he **admit / deny / report** — **breaking** the window?

We **considered / suggested / postponed** — **taking** a trip.

The **-ing** form of the verb can be used as the object of certain verbs: **admit, avoid, consider, deny, enjoy, finish, imagine, mind, miss, postpone, practice, recommend, report,** and **suggest**.

PRACTICE

Answer the questions according to the pictures and using the -ing form of the verb.

EX. What do young people enjoy?
  ▷ **They enjoy dancing.**

*(+)I suggest going to (어디어디?)
[→] I don't suggest going to (")*

1. What does Mr. Ferrara avoid?

▷

He avoid washing dishses

2. What did Kenny postpone?

▷

~~Kenny~~ He postponed doing hw.

3. What did the little girl deny?

▷

she deny breaking the window
I didn't doing.

ex) I am considering going to London.
고려하고생각하다 [S/W] → Think

4. What is Mrs. Hu considering for her next vacation?

▷

She's considering camping,
going
(= go camping.)

5. What did Boris suggest?

▷

He suggested eating
in a restaurant

Verb (+) infinitive or gerund
Usually
experience 때에 쓸때는 "have" 강조이 또다

STUDY 3

The **to** infinitive or the **-ing** form of the verb as objects:
I don't like going out in groups. I don't like to go out in groups.

Notice the main verbs and the forms that follow them.

Usually
past about
future a

I
| like
started
began
tried
continued |

| to swim
swimming | in the ocean.

The verbs **begin, continue, hate, like, love, prefer, start,** and **try**
can be used with either the **to** infinitive or the **-ing** form of the
verb.

PRACTICE

**Complete the sentences according to the pictures. First give the _-ing_
form of the verb. Then give the _to_ infinitive.**

EX. Paul likes __playing soccer__.
I like __to play soccer__, too.

same meaning

1. Alice prefers ___Playing basketball___.
likes
Julia prefers ___to play soccer___, too.

2. Susan hates _____cleaning in her room_____. *(vacuuming)*
Do you hate _____to clean in her room_____, too?

3. It just started _____raining_____.
It always starts _____to rain_____
at this time.

skating? 2ʸ ground after 6 ʸ

4. Everyone tried _____ice skating_____.
Even I tried _____to skate_____.

tenins

5. I love _____playing_____.
Do you love _____to play_____, too?

tenine

runing (fast)

6. I've been _____jogging (slower)_____ every day.
You should begin _____to jog_____, too.

run

⚹ What do you remember playing as a child?

➔ I remember ~~playing~~ *playing soccer*
(swimming)

LISTEN

A. Listen carefully to the information. Then choose the statement that is true according to the information you have heard.

1. a. Barbara read the article in half an hour.
    b. Barbara read the article twice.
    c. Barbara read the article in two hours.

2. a. The play is interesting.
    b. The play is not popular.
    c. The play is popular.

3. a. The girls told the truth.
    b. The girls didn't tell the truth.
    c. The girls don't know the truth.

4. a. I don't like swimming at the lake.
    b. I like swimming, but not at the lake.
    c. I like swimming at the lake.

5. a. Tom smokes.
    b. Tom doesn't smoke.
    c. Tom's doctor smokes.

6. a. Karen wants to play tennis.
    b. Karen doesn't want to play tennis now.
    c. Karen doesn't like to play tennis.

B. Listen carefully to the information. Then choose the correct answer.

1. a. To the mountains.
    b. To the country.
    c. To the beach.

2. a. On 14th Street.
    b. On 23rd Street.
    c. On Barrow Street.

3. a. She teaches accounting.
    b. She teaches economics.
    c. She teaches sailing.

4. a. Going shopping.
    b. Staying home.
    c. Going to the movies.

READ

Entertainment at No Cost

Most of us think entertainment costs money. Movies, concerts, and shows are enjoyable but expensive. If you think that you can't have a good time without spending a lot of money, read on. A little thinking and a few minutes of newspaper scanning should give you some pleasant surprises.

People may be the most interesting show in a large city. Walk the busy streets and see what everybody else is doing. You will probably see people from all over the world; you will certainly see people of every age, size, and shape; and you'll get a free fashion show, too. Window-shopping is also a safe sport—if the stores are closed.

Check the listings in your neighborhood paper. Local colleges or schools often welcome the public to hear an interesting speaker or see a good performance. The film or concert series at the local public library or museum probably won't cost you a penny. Be sure to check business advertising, too. A flea market can provide hours of pleasant browsing. Perhaps you can find a free cooking or crafts demonstration in a department store.

How about some outdoor music? Street musicians are usually delighted to have an appreciative audience even if you can't afford to throw a dime or a quarter into their hats. On a good day, you may have your choice of classical, rock, folk, blues, or bluegrass music, plus a lot of warm sunshine and fresh air. Magicians, mimes, jugglers, clowns, acrobats, and dancers sometimes put on free shows, too. To find these performances, look where many people walk—for example, near stores, theaters, and bus and train stations. Try the city parks, too.

Plan ahead for some activities. It is always more pleasant not to have people in front of you in a museum or at the zoo. You may save money, too, since these places often set aside one or two free-admission days at slow times during the week.

Pretend from time to time that you are a tourist, and get to know your city well. See the sights that people travel long distances to see. Find a free walking tour, or plan one yourself with the help of a guidebook. You will see your city in a new light once you know more about its history and architecture.

It is not difficult to create your own fun. Newspaper articles and ads can give you new ideas each week. By taking part in these activities, you may meet people who share your interests. Through these people, you will learn about many activities that are not listed in any newspaper. With imagination and a spirit of adventure, you can easily find entertainment at no cost at all.

Answer and Discuss

1. What kinds of entertainment cost money?
2. What can you see just by walking the streets of a large city?
3. How can a newspaper help you find free activities?
4. What kinds of free concerts can be found outdoors?
5. Who else often performs outdoors?
6. Where can you find these outdoor performers?
7. What places often offer free admission on certain days?
8. What is the advantage of pretending to be a tourist?
9. How can new friends help you find free entertainment?
10. What free entertainment can you find in your city?

PHRASAL VERBS

Come up with, turn down, and turn up

Notice the meaning of these phrasal verbs.

One day, David **turned up** at the library to talk to Ling.
David asked her to go out with him, but she **turned** him **down**.
If he invites her again, she'll **turn down** the invitation again.
She can always **come up with** a good excuse in these situations.

Come up with (nonseparable) is a three-word phrasal verb meaning "produce."
Turn down (separable) means "refuse, reject."
Turn up means "appear." It does not take a direct object.

PRACTICE

Complete the sentences using the correct form of an appropriate verb from the following list.

come	turn	turn up
come up with	turn down	

1. My friend June _____ to our company for a job interview yesterday.

2. The head of personnel interviewed June and offered her a job, but he couldn't _____ a high enough salary.

3. June liked the job, but _____ it _____ because of the salary.

4. After the interview, June _____ at my office. She asked me if I knew about any other openings.

5. I couldn't _____ any suggestions.

6. So June thanked me, _____, and walked out of my office.

THINK AND SPEAK

Look over the possibilities for community activities listed in this copy of a Monday newspaper. Plan your week. Invite another student to go somewhere with you. You will each pay for your own tickets. Try to choose some free activities to avoid spending a lot of money.

Guide to Weekend Entertainment	
Hancock Historical Museum: Costumes of the 18th Century. Open Sat. and Sun. 10:00–4:00. Adults $1.00; children $.50.	Riverside Park: Canoe and boat rental, $2/hr. from 9–6 Sat. and Sun. Boat races 2 P.M. Sunday; admission free.

Greenville Zoo. Open daily from 10:00–6:00. Admission free.	Saturday Movies at the YMCA:
	  6:30–"City Lights" with Charlie Chaplin
	  8:30–"Mata Hari" with Greta Garbo
	  10:30–"Jaws" with Roy Scheider
	Tickets to each show: $1.50.

Johnson Memorial Park: Bicycle rental from 8:00–8:00. $1.50 per hour; $4.00 all day. ———•——— Band Concert Sunday 5:00–7:00 P.M. Admission free. ———•——— Free Nature Trail Walk with Botanist Dr. Jean Mulligan. Meet at Park Information Bureau at 9:00 A.M. Walk takes 3 hours. ———•——— Picnic grounds open 8:00–8:00.	Soccer Match at Malek Stadium: Sat. 6:00 P.M. Greenville vs. Hancock; adults $5, children $2.

VOCABULARY EXPANSION

The prefixes **over-/under-**, **up-/down-**, and **in-/out-**

Notice the meaning and formation of these words.

too much — | **over-** | + | charge / estimate | = | **overcharge** / **overestimate**

Not enough — | **under-** | + | charge / estimate | = | **undercharge** / **underestimate**

The tomatoes cost $1.99 a pound. The clerk charged me $2.99.
The clerk **overcharged** me.

The bread cost $1.69. The clerk charged me $.69.
The clerk **undercharged** me.

I thought it would take me a week to paint my house.
It took me two weeks to paint my house.
I **underestimated** the time it would take me to paint my house.

I thought I would owe $2,000 in taxes, but I owed $1,200.
I **overestimated** the amount I would owe in taxes.

| **up-** | + | stairs / hill | = | **upstairs** / **uphill** |

| **down-** | + | stairs / hill | = | **downstairs** / **downhill** |

I was on the first floor. I took the stairs to the second floor.
I went **upstairs**.

I was on the second floor. I took the stairs to the first floor.
I went **downstairs**.

We rode our bicycles from the bottom to the top of the hill.
We rode **uphill**.

We rode our bicycles from the top to the bottom of the hill.
We rode **downhill**.

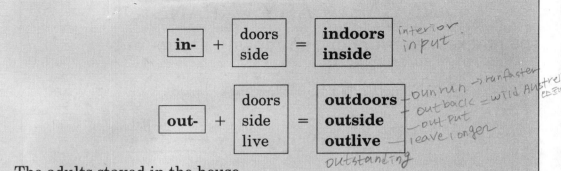

The adults stayed in the house.
The children went out to play in the yard.
The adults stayed **indoors**.
The children went **outdoors**.

Roberto was going to meet José at the library.
They didn't find each other.
Roberto was waiting **outside**.
José was waiting **inside**.

Mr. Lee lived longer than any of his brothers.
He **outlived** them.

The prefix **over-** means "too much, more than normal."
The prefix **under-** means "not enough, less than normal."
The prefix **up-** means "higher."
The prefix **down-** means "lower."
The prefix **in-** means "interior, directed to the center."
The prefix **out-** means "exterior, directed away from the center." It can also mean "more, faster, or longer," as in **outlive**.

PRACTICE

Complete each sentence using the correct form of one of these words.

downhill	inwardly	overestimate	upstairs
downstairs	outdoors	underestimate	upward
indoors	outrun	uphill	

1. Max loves to watch TV, read, and clean house. He spends most of his weekends _indoors_.

2. His neighbor Anne loves to play tennis, swim, and run. She spends most of her weekends _outdoors_.

3. Anne can easily _outrun_ runners who are younger than she is.

4. It's easy for Anne to run _downhill_, but she also enjoys running _uphill_.

5. Playing tennis, she _underestimate_ her strength and hits the ball harder than she needs to.

6. She _overestimate_ Max's patience. He gets angry very fast.

7. One day, Max was sitting _upstairs_ looking down at Anne practicing tennis next door.

8. Suddenly a tennis ball flew _upward_ and broke the window of the room where Max was sitting.

9. Max raced _downstairs_ to tell Anne what he thought about her tennis.

10. On the outside, he appeared calm, but _____, he was furious.

with 아이에 전이어가

PRONOUNCE: [ž] [jz]

leisure	friction between tongue and palate, voiced

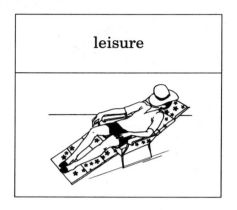
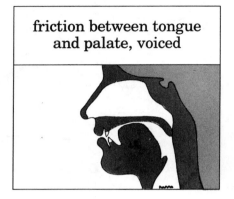

A. Repeat the following words.

발음 그게어에게

Asia	decision	mirage	treasure
casual	garage [예]	pleasure	usual
confusion	measure [애]	television	version

B. On a sheet of paper, write the numbers of the words that contain the [ž] sound.

1. seizure
2. vision
3. surprise ∝ᄀ
4. measure
5. delicious [✗ᄀ

6. usual
7. leisure
8. advantage [✗ᄀ
9. confusion
10. treasure

11. pleasure
12. version
13. casual
14. television
15. mirage

C. Listen to this saying and repeat it.

Everyone enjoys leisure time. Benjamin has leisure time after school, and he likes to watch television. Jane and George find leisure time on weekends. They put on causal clothes and go on excursions. Jean has some leisure time in the evening. She likes to read magazines. Leisure time is for pleasure.

D. Listen to this saying and repeat it.

Marry in haste, suffer at leisure.

CONVERSATION

Friday the Thirteenth = Bad luck
= superstition → something you believe that has no reason.

Michael, Mario, and Sarah are planning to go to a football game with a group of other people from the office where they work. Michael isn't sure he wants to go with them.

MICHAEL: How many people from the office are going to the game?

MARIO: Thirteen, I think.

MICHAEL: Thirteen? And today is Friday the thirteenth! I don't think I'll go with you.

MARIO: Why not? Are you superstitious?

MICHAEL: Not really. I'd already decided not to go. But everybody knows that Friday and thirteen sometimes bring you bad luck.

MARIO: You really are superstitious! Do you think it's bad luck to break a mirror, too?

MICHAEL: Well, I broke my arm once right after I'd broken a mirror.

MARIO: So what? The mirror had nothing to do with the arm. It was just a coincidence.

MICHAEL: Maybe it was. But there are a few things that definitely bring bad luck. Why do you think so many hotels don't have a thirteenth floor?

MARIO: Because people like you refuse to stay on the thirteenth floor!

SARAH: Calm down, you two. It's ridiculous for you to argue about this. Everyone has a few superstitions—even you, Mario. Just the other day I saw you avoid walking under a ladder.

MARIO: You know, you're right. I did it without even thinking.

Answer and Discuss

1. Why doesn't Michael want to go to the football game?
2. Do you believe that Michael had already decided not to go? *At the moment*
3. When did Michael break his arm? *After broken mirro* *p.p 요절*
4. Does Mario think there was a relation between Michael's broken arm and the broken mirror? *He just a concidence*
5. Why don't many hotels have a thirteenth floor, according to Michael? According to Mario? *(a) 싫어하는*
6. Who tries to stop the argument? How is she able to stop it? *Sarah*
7. Do you think that Mario is superstitious, too? *yes. =he avoiding walking under a ladder*

INTERACTION

A. Discuss the following situation and questions with a partner or with the class.

Some people believe that breaking a mirror will bring you seven years of bad luck. Other people think that walking under a ladder or opening an umbrella indoors brings bad luck. Many people also believe that it's good luck to find a four-leaf clover and that carrying a rabbit's foot or displaying a horseshoe brings good luck. Do you know about these superstitions? What superstitions are common in your country? Do you have any superstitions? What are they?

B. Read the following situation. Then, with a partner, play one of the roles described.

Two friends are planning a party for Friday night. But that Friday falls on the thirteenth of the month.

1. You are planning a party for the thirteenth. You are not superstitious and do not understand people who are.
2. You are helping your friend to plan the party. But you don't think that Friday the thirteenth is the best day for it because some people are superstitious. They may hesitate to attend. Try to persuade your friend to change the day of the party.

- adverbs often come between the first part the second part + (had never met t)

(had + P.P) ex) I had never met an American until now.

STUDY 1

The past perfect tense: *I'd already decided not to go.*

including two action same time - past ½ one action ...

Notice the formation of the past perfect tense.

had pp + simple past = action 1 action 2 action

I			
You		**cleaned**	the house
He	**had**	**bought**	the food
She	**'d**	**made**	a pie
We		**prepared**	dinner
They		**washed**	the dishes
		set	the table

before the guests arrived.

The past perfect tense expresses a past time occurring before another past time.

(happen)

Form the past perfect tense with **had + the past participle of the main verb**.

past have

The contraction of **had** is **'d**.

The negative of the past perfect tense is formed with **hadn't**.
> We'd prepared dinner before the guests arrived, but we **hadn't eaten** yet.

Already, just, and adverbs of frequency like **never** are usually placed between **had** and the past participle.
> I'd **never** met the guests before, but my parents had **already** met them several times. My brother had **just** met them the week before.

I just finish. one second ago

1) ⇒ Completed Action Before Something in past.

past — present — future
Past Perfect
Presnt still now.
continue

before had+ p.p. ↗ ~~그것을 말고~~

a *religious* teacher 종교적인

PRACTICE

Complete the sentences using the past perfect form of the verb in parentheses.

ex ─────┼──────────┼──────────┼── Now
He cleaned   Guests
               arrives.

Ristorante Regina

Past Perfect
Past of past
different time

EX. John visited Rome in August. He knew Rome well because he
__had been__ there many times. (be)

1. John had an old friend named Kathy there. He ___had known___ her
for many years. (know)

2. John invited Kathy and her husband Carlo to go out to lunch with
him. He chose the Ristorante Regina, a restaurant where he
___had eaten___ many times. (eat)

3. At three o'clock John called Kathy up to see if they wanted to walk
to the restaurant with him, but they ___had___ (already)
___left___ their apartment. (leave)

4. John went directly to the restaurant. Kathy and Carlo
___had promised___ to meet him there at half past three. (promise)

5. John didn't get there until twenty to four, but Kathy and Carlo
___had gotten___ there only a few minutes earlier. (get)

6. John enjoyed talking to Carlo. He ___had___ never
___met___ him before. (meet)

STUDY 2

Tense sequence in the past:
I broke my arm once right after I'd broken a mirror.

Notice the use of the past and past perfect tenses.

I | **called,** | but Susan | **had** | already | **left**.

The past tense refers to an action completed in the past.
The past perfect tense refers to an action which occurred before
another past action.

⊟ PRACTICE

A. Fill in each blank with the past or past perfect form of the verb in parentheses. If a second word is given after the verb, use that word in the sentence, too.

I _____went_____ (go) to Paris in 1988. I

had never been (be) (never) there

before. When I ___saw___ (see) the

Eiffel Tower with my own eyes, I

_____was_____ (be) delighted. It

_____was_____ (be) nothing like the

pictures I ___had seen___ (see)! I even

remembered (remember) a little of

my high-school French which I

_____thought_____ (think) I

had forgotten (forget).

I saw pictures 1980

It was nothing.

forgot French #1   *I thought #2*   *now*

B. Complete the sentences with the past or past perfect form of the verb in parentheses. If a second word is given after the verb, use that word in the sentence, too.

SOLD OUT

EX. Maria **wanted** to see the new play in town. (want)

1. She _____ me to go see it with her. (invite)

2. I didn't want to go because I _____ it. (see) (already)

3. Then Maria _____ Lin to go with her. (ask)

4. Lin couldn't go because she ~~did~~ had already made other plans. (make) (already)

5. Paul, however, hadn't seen it yet. (see) (not)

6. Maria and Paul went to the theater to buy tickets. (go)

7. Unfortunately, the woman at the ticket window had just sold the last one. (sell) (just)

8. Maria and Paul came to see me after they left the theater. (come)

9. They _____ very disappointed. (be)

10. They were upset because they had had really such bad luck that day. (have)

LISTEN

A. Listen carefully to the information. Then choose the statement that is true according to the information you have heard.

1. a. Tim does not play soccer.
   b. Tim plays soccer badly.
   c. Tim plays soccer well.

2. a. It took us two extra hours to get home.
   b. It usually takes two hours to get home.
   c. It usually takes longer than two hours to get home.

3. a. Carl was still at the hotel.
   b. Carl was still checking out of the hotel.
   c. Carl had already left the hotel.

4. a. She planned to go.
   b. She did not go.
   c. She went.

5. a. Martha saw the spelling mistakes before Linda.
   b. Linda saw the spelling mistakes first.
   c. Linda corrected the spelling mistakes.

6. a. George stopped the fight.
   b. Ken and Frank were fighting with George.
   c. George ran outside because he wanted to watch the fight.

B. Listen carefully to the information. Then choose the correct answer.

1. a. In Colombia.
   b. In Italy.
   c. In Venezuela.

2. a. It's five o'clock.
   b. It's earlier than five o'clock.
   c. It's later than five o'clock.

3. a. An accountant.
   b. A secretary.
   c. A businesswoman.

4. a. At a restaurant.
   b. At a grocery store.
   c. At work.

READ

How to Improve Your Study Habits

Maybe you are an average student with an average intellect. You pass most of your subjects. You occasionally get good grades, but they are usually just average. You are more interested in hiking than in history and in sports than in scholarship. The fact is that you don't study very much.

You probably think you will never be a top student. This is not necessarily so, however. Anyone can become a better scholar if he or she wants to. It is true that you may not be enthusiastic about everything you study, but by using your time properly you may improve your grades without additional work. Here's how.

1. *Plan your time carefully.* When you plan a trip, one of the first things you must do is to make a list of things to take. If you don't, you are almost certain to leave something important at home. When you plan your week, you should make a list of things that you have to do. Otherwise, you may forget to leave enough time to complete an important task. After making the list, you should make a schedule of your time. First fill in committed time—eating, sleeping, dressing,

school, meetings, and so forth. Then decide on a good, regular time for studying. Be sure to set aside enough time to complete the work that you are normally assigned each week. Of course, studying shouldn't occupy all of your free time. Don't forget to set aside enough time for entertainment, hobbies, and maybe just relaxation. A weekly schedule may not solve all your problems, but it will force you to realize what is happening to your time.

2. *Find a good place to study.* Look around the house for a good study area. Keep this space, which may be a desk or simply a corner of your room, free of everything but study materials. No games, radios, or television! If you can't find such a place at home, find a library where you can study. When you sit down to work, concentrate on the subject! And don't go to the place you have chosen unless you are ready to study.

3. *Make good use of your time in class.* Take advantage of class time to listen to everything the teacher says. Sit where you can see and hear well. Really listening in class means less work later. Taking notes will help you remember what the teacher says. When the teacher gets off the subject, stop taking notes.

4. *Study regularly.* When you get home from class, go over your notes. Review the important points that your teacher mentioned in class. Read any related material in your textbook. If you know what your teacher is going to discuss the next day, scan and read that material, too. This will help you understand the next class. If you do these things regularly, the material will become more meaningful, and you will remember it longer. ~~to go throw it~~ You very carefuly

5. *Scan before you read.* This means looking a passage over quickly but thoroughly before you begin to read it more carefully. Scanning a passage lets you preview the material and get a general idea of the content. This will actually allow you to skip less important material when you begin to read. Scanning will help you double your reading speed and improve your comprehension.

6. *Develop a good attitude about tests.* The purpose of a test is to show what you have learned about a subject. The world won't end if you don't pass a test, so don't get overly worried. Tests do more than just provide grades; they let you know what you need to study more, and they help make your new knowledge permanent. Forever.

   There are other techniques that might help you with your studying. Only a handful have been mentioned here. You will probably discover many others after you have tried these.

   → [Thur – row – Lee]

Answer and Discuss

1. Can an average student become a better scholar?
2. Why is it important to make a weekly schedule of your time?
3. Should you spend all your free time studying? What other activities should you set aside time for?
4. What kind of place should you choose as a study area?
5. How can you make good use of your time in class? 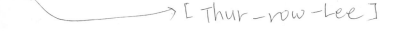 Dont leave early ~~or then~~
6. Should you write down everything the teacher says?
7. What should you do every day when you get home from class?
8. How does scanning help you study?
9. What is the purpose of a test?
10. Which one of the suggestions will help you the most?

PHRASAL VERBS

Break up, **point out**, and **walk out on**

Notice the meaning of these phrasal verbs.

Mehmet tried to **break up** the argument between Susanna and Ramón. He had already **pointed out** that it was time to change the subject, but Susanna was so upset that she **walked out on** both of them.

Break up (separable) means "put a stop to."
Point out (separable) means "bring to (someone's) attention."
Walk out on (nonseparable) means "leave" (someone).

PRACTICE

Complete the sentences using the correct form of an appropriate verb from the following list.

point out	walk out on	break up
point	walk	break

1. Timothy ___broke___ Mark's pen.

2. Mark ___pointed___ at him and shouted, "You should buy me another one!"

3. Timothy ___pointed out___ that it was just a cheap pen.

4. He then started to ___walk___ toward the door.

5. Mark asked, "Are you going to ___walk out on___ me without paying for the pen?" "That's right," said Timothy.

6. Then Mark hit Timothy. Luckily, Carl came in and ___broke up___ the fight.

THINK AND SPEAK

What should this student do to improve her study habits? How are your study habits different from hers?

VOCABULARY EXPANSION

The suffixes -ful and -ship

Notice the meaning and formation of these words.

I recently purchased a **membership** in a cooking club. There I learned that food should look **beautiful** as well as taste delicious. I learned that the key to good baking is being **careful** about measuring the ingredients. If a recipe calls for a **cupful** of flour, the instructor told us to use a measuring cup to get the exact amount. It's also important to know whether a **spoonful** in a recipe is a **teaspoonful** or a **tablespoonful**. A **handful** isn't an exact amount and wouldn't be used in a recipe. I'm very **thankful** to the instructor. He has made cooking and baking seem easy and fun. I've also made some new **friendships** with the other club members.

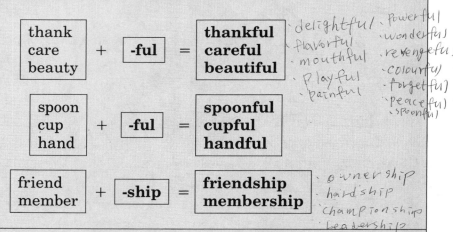

| thank care beauty | + | -ful | = | thankful careful beautiful |

delightful · powerful
· flavorful · wonderful
· mouthful · revengeful
· playful · colourful
· painful · forgetful
· peaceful
· spoonful

| spoon cup hand | + | -ful | = | spoonful cupful handful |

| friend member | + | -ship | = | friendship membership |

· ownership
hardship
championship
· leadership

The (suffix) -ful means "full of" (something) or "enough to fill" (something). → *y* at the end of the word

The suffix **-ship** means "the state, fact, or concept of" (something). If a word ends in **y**, change the **y** to **i** before adding the suffix.

beauty + –ful = **beautiful**

PRACTICE

Complete the story by filling in the suffix missing from each word: *-ful* or *-ship*.

On November 16, 1963, archaeologists began a large project near Lake Nasser in Egypt. They started the care_____ removal of the two temples of Rameses to a higher and safer spot. The leader_____ of two famous archaeologists made the project possible. The two scientists shared a deep friend_____ and had an ideal partner_____. In addition, they both had an excellent relation_____ with the engineers and workers on the project. Everyone was very hope_____ that their plan would be a success.

Power_____ cranes moved tons and tons of rock. The workers tried to be as help_____ as possible. They sifted through each arm_____ of debris and were watch_____ to be sure to keep every fragment of the temples. Some of the workers were students. A scholar_____ program paid their travel and living expenses. Visitors to the scene were often surprised to find a whole room_____ of archaeologists discussing the project in a nearby building.

The team finished its work on the Great Temple in the autumn of 1967. Through the thought_____ planning and care_____ efforts of those involved, the beauti_____ temples were at last safe from the rising waters of Lake Nasser. Everyone was thank_____ when the project turned out to be success_____.

PRONOUNCE

Initial consonant clusters with s-

[sk-]	[skr-]	[sl-]	[sm-]	[sn-]
scan	scream	slow	small	snow
school	Scrabble	sleep	smart	snake
scholarship	scratch	slender	Smith	sneeze

[sp-]	[spl-]	[spr-]	[st-]	[str-]
space	split	sprain	start	street
speed	splash	spring	stop	strong
sports	splendid	sprinkle	study	strokes

A. Listen to these words. On a sheet of paper, write the letter of the word that you hear in each pair.

1. a. smoke	b. soak	6. a. slice	b. lice
2. a. snow	b. stow	7. a. speak	b. peak
3. a. skit	b. split	8. a. slash	b. splash
4. a. cream	b. scream	9. a. star	b. tar
5. a. sleep	b. steep	10. a. stop	b. slop

B. Listen to this saying and repeat it.

Steve is both smart and scholarly. He starts studying right after dinner and doesn't stop until he goes to sleep. He's also a sports star. Although slender and small, he's both a runner and a swimmer. He runs with great speed and swims with strong strokes.

C. Listen to this saying and repeat it.

Small sorrows speak, great ones are silent.

CONVERSATION

Volunteer Work

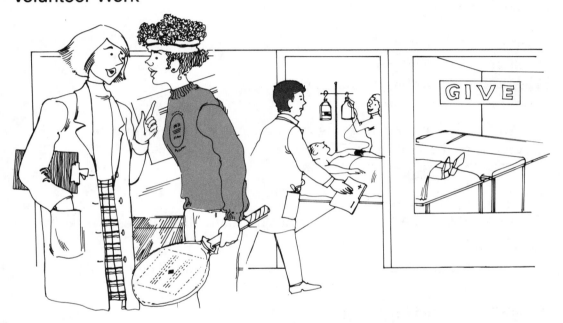

Ann is working as a volunteer at the hospital blood bank. Carmen has come to donate blood and stops to talk to Ann.

CARMEN: What are you doing here?

ANN: I'm working.

CARMEN: So you got a job!

ANN: Well, yes. It's volunteer work.

105

CARMEN: Oh—if you're just a volunteer, why don't you leave early, and play tennis with us? We're going to those nice new courts near the stadium.

ANN: I can't leave yet. I have to work three more hours this afternoon.

CARMEN: What about tomorrow?

ANN: Tomorrow I'm going to visit some elderly people here in the hospital.

CARMEN: Listen, Ann, you shouldn't do so much volunteer work. The hospital is just taking advantage of you. They should pay you for this work.

ANN: But the hospital doesn't have enough money to pay me.

CARMEN: Maybe the government would find enough money for hospitals if fewer people worked for free.

ANN: Well, I don't care about the money. And I really feel this is an educational experience.

Answer and Discuss

1. Where is Ann working?
2. Is it a regular job?
3. What does Carmen invite Ann to do?
4. Where are she and her friends going to play tennis?
5. Why can't Ann leave the blood bank yet?
6. Why can't she play tennis tomorrow, either?
7. What does Carmen think of volunteer work?
8. What does Ann think of volunteer work?
9. Have you ever worked as a volunteer? Tell the class about it.

INTERACTION

A. Discuss the following questions with a partner or with the class.

1. Is it a good idea to do volunteer work?
2. Does volunteer work take jobs from people who need them?
3. Does volunteer work benefit the volunteers?

B. Read the following situation. Then, with a partner, play one of the roles described.

A tour of a local park led by a ranger is going to take place this Saturday.

1. A friend invites you to go on the tour. But you are a volunteer at a local school for the handicapped, and you have promised to help take the children to the zoo that day. You get satisfaction from helping the children and the teachers. Try to explain this to your friend.
2. Your friend has said he or she can't go on the tour because he or she is doing volunteer work with handicapped children on Saturday. You think that volunteers take work from teachers and aides who need jobs. Try to persuade your friend that you are right.

STUDY 1

Series of adjectives as modifiers of a noun:
We're going to those nice new courts near the stadium.

Notice the position of different types of adjectives.

Determiner	General	Size	Age	Color	Nationality	Noun
...a		**tall**	**young**		**Dominican**	woman.
...the	**nice**	**big**		**blue**	*English*	house.
...that	**nice**	**little**			**Italian**	store.
...my	**ugly**		**old**	**green**	*Chinses*	car.

(handwritten above "General": opinion)
(handwritten below Nationality column: International)

Determiners precede adjectives. General adjectives are followed by adjectives of size, age, color, and nationality, in that order. Commas are often placed between adjectives, especially those of the same category.

I just bought some **nice, sweet** strawberries.

 # PRACTICE

Complete the sentences with the words given in parentheses. Be sure to put the words in the correct order.

EX. Paulo was **a smart Brazilian boy.** (Brazilian, smart, boy, a)
1. He got lost in _a big ~~modern~~ city_. (city, modern, big, a)
2. He found _a nice young police officer_. (police officer, young, a, nice)
3. The police officer took him to _his big white house_. (white, his, house, big)
4. _A small blond boy_ came out of the house. (a, blond, boy, small)
5. He was playing with _a large red ball_. (red, large, ball, a)
6. Paulo played with the boy until his parents arrived in _a small Japanese car_. (Japanese, car, a, small)

STUDY 2

Series of nouns as modifiers of a noun:
Ann is a volunteer hospital worker.

Notice the use of the noun modifiers.

Ann is a | **volunteer** | worker.

Ann is a | **hospital** | worker.

Ann is a | **volunteer hospital** | worker.

A series of <u>nouns can modify another noun</u>. Adjectives are placed before the series of noun modifiers.

PRACTICE

Complete the sentences with the words in parentheses. Be sure to put the words in the correct order.

EX. There was a fire in an <u>old retirement home</u>. (home, retirement, old)

1. I was a _____. (firefighter, volunteer, new)
2. We went to the fire in a _____. (engine, fire, noisy)
3. We got to the fire by using an _____. (old, road, fire)
4. We unrolled the _____. (hose, long, fire)
5. We connected the hose to the _____.
   (fire, hydrant, nearest)
6. Some _____ were blocking the road.
   (uniformed, police officers, state)
7. I broke down the door of the _____
   (room, basement, recreation)
8. A man was lying on the _____. (cement, hard, floor)
9. He was one of the _____.
   (home, employees, retirement)
10. We carried him to the _____. (ambulance, new, white)

[handwritten margin notes: Adverbs of Time / 1) She tries to get back before dark / 2) It's starting to get dark now / 3) she left early / 4) she finished her test first / Place]

STUDY 3

Adverbs as modifiers of nouns:
We're going to those nice new courts near the stadium.

[handwritten margin notes: she still live there now / the girl next to / Cristina is ...]

Notice the meaning and position of the adverbial modifiers.

The tennis courts are nice. They're **near the stadium**.

The tennis courts | **near the stadium** | are nice.

The girl is Carmen. She's **next to Ann**.

The girl | **next to Ann** | is Carmen.

Ann and Carmen had a conversation **today**. It was interesting.

Their conversation | **today** | was interesting.

Some adverbial expressions of place and time may occur after a noun to modify it. The adverb may be a word or a prepositional phrase.

[handwritten: noun ... adverb of place or time ...]

PRACTICE

A. Expand each sentence by using the adverb in parentheses as a modifier of the noun.

[handwritten margin notes: Adverbs →describe how the verb act / answer/Qestion / next to / near / there / every where]

EX.   The big house is ours. (next to the lake)
▷   **The big house next to the lake is ours.**

1.   The boat belongs to a neighbor. (on the lake)
▷   *The boat (on the lake) belongs to a neighbor [adverb]*

[handwritten margin notes: How, where, when →before now / first / (usually end in -ly) / early]

2.   The big garden keeps us busy. (in the back)
▷

3.   The five rooms are sunny and large. (upstairs)
▷

4.   The homeowners are friendly and pleasant. (around us)
▷   *the homeowners around us are friendly and pleasant.*

5.   The neighbors are like members of the family. (on the corner)
▷   *The neighbors on the corner are like members of the family*

B. Combine these sentences as in the example. Use the adverb as a modifier of the noun.

EX. There's a travel agency near my house. I went to the travel agency for information on inexpensive vacations.

▷ **I went to the travel agency near my house for information on inexpensive vacations.**

1. There's a travel agent at the desk. The travel agent gave me several suggestions.

▷

2. There are tours to the Caribbean. The tours are a lot of fun.

▷

3. There are mountains on the Caribbean islands. The mountains are beautiful.

▷

4. There are beaches there. The beaches are very sandy.

▷

5. There's going to be a tour next month. The tour is very inexpensive.

▷

6. There are also tours during the winter. The tours are a little more expensive.

▷

LISTEN

A. Listen carefully to the information. Then choose the statement that is true according to the information you have heard.

1. a. Francis went to the hotel by car.
   b. Francis went to the hotel by bus.
   c. Francis came to the city by bus.

2. a. Kim was driving at the right speed.
   b. Kim was driving too slowly.
   c. Kim was driving too fast.

3. a. It's 9:15.
   b. It's 9:30.
   c. It's 9:45.

4. a. The baby ate six times a day.
   b. The baby ate four times a day.
   c. The baby ate eight times a day.

5. a. John arrived before Carmen.
   b. John arrived at eleven o'clock.
   c. John arrived at nine o'clock.

6. a. It's about nine o'clock.
   b. It's about ten o'clock.
   c. It's about five o'clock.

B. Listen carefully to the information. Then choose the correct answer.

1. a. Thirty dollars.
   b. Thirteen dollars.
   c. Three dollars.

2. a. At a bank.
   b. At a restaurant.
   c. At a supermarket.

3. a. Seventeen dollars.
   b. Thirty-four dollars.
   c. Eighteen dollars and fifty cents.

4. a. The more comfortable one.
   b. The new one.
   c. The older one.

READ

The Tortoise and the Hare

A hare met a tortoise one day and made fun of him because of the slow and clumsy way he walked.

The tortoise laughed and said, "I will race you any time."

"Very well," replied the hare. "We will start at once."

The tortoise immediately set off in his slow but steady pace without waiting a moment or looking back. The hare, on the other hand, treated the matter as a joke and decided to take a little nap before starting. He thought it would be easy to overtake the tortoise.

The tortoise plodded on. Meanwhile, the hare overslept. As a result, the hare arrived at the finish line only to see that the tortoise had arrived before him.

Slow and steady wins the race.

Answer and Discuss

1. Why did the hare make fun of the tortoise?
2. What did they decide to do?
3. How did the tortoise begin the race?
4. Why did the hare take a nap?
5. Why did the hare lose the race?
6. What lesson can you learn from this fable?

Aesop's Fables

People all over the world are familiar with the fables attributed to Aesop. For over nine hundred years these stories were told and retold before they were finally written down in the third century A.D. They are full of useful advice for people everywhere.

Belling the Cat

Long ago, some mice had a meeting to consider what they could do to outwit their enemy, the cat. They discussed the merits of many plans. At last, a young mouse got up and said that she had a good solution to the problem.

"You will agree," she said, "that our greatest danger is the sly manner in which our enemy approaches us. If we could receive warning of her approach, we could easily escape from her. I suggest, therefore, that a small bell be tied around the neck of the cat. In this way, we will always know when she is coming, and we can easily run away."

Everyone thought this was an excellent plan. But at that moment, a wise old mouse got up and said, "That is all very well, but who is going to bell the cat?" The mice looked at each other and nobody spoke. Then the wise old mouse said, "It is easy to suggest impossible solutions."

It is one thing to propose, another to execute.

Answer and Discuss

1. What danger was facing the mice?
2. Who spoke up first?
3. What did the young mouse suggest?
4. What did the wise old mouse say?
5. Have you had an experience like this? Tell about it.

The Wind and the Sun

The North Wind and the Sun once had an argument about which of them was stronger. Unable to agree, they decided to try to see which one could make a traveler on the road take off his coat.

The North Wind started the contest, sending a strong blast of cold air to blow the coat away. However, instead of taking off his coat, the traveler wrapped it around his body more closely than ever.

The Sun laughed at the North Wind's failure. Then, using all his power, the Sun sent its warm beams down to earth and drove the thick, heavy clouds from the sky. Feeling warmer and warmer, the traveler began to slow down. He began to perspire. He felt weaker and weaker. Finally, unable to endure it any longer, the traveler took off his coat and sat down in the shade of some nearby trees.

Persuasion is better than force.

Answer and Discuss

1. What did the North Wind and the Sun have an argument about?
2. How did they decide to settle the argument?
3. What did the North Wind do?
4. What did the traveler do then?
5. What did the Sun do?
6. What did the traveler do then?
7. Tell about a time when you learned that persuasion is better than force.

PHRASAL VERBS

Make fun of, get back at, and take (something) out on

Notice the meaning of these phrasal verbs.

Some people **make fun of** Ann because she does so much volunteer work. But even though Ann gets angry, she never tries to **get back at** these people, and she never **takes it out on** anyone else.

Make fun of (nonseparable) means "ridicule" or "laugh at."
Get back at (nonseparable) means "take revenge on." Vendetta
Take (something) out on (separable) means "abuse (someone) by venting one's anger or frustration." The direct object **it** often replaces the idea of anger or frustration.

He took **his anger** out on her. → He took **it** out on her.

Don't take it out on me

PRACTICE

Complete the sentences using the correct form of an appropriate verb from the list below.

make fun of	take it out on	get back at
make	take	get

1. Charles went home and began to scream at his sister. He'd had a bad day at the office, and now he was _____ her.

2. He was upset because some people were _____ him at the office. They were laughing at his bright red tie.

3. Now he's thinking of a way to _____ them. Charles believes in revenge.

4. Instead, he should _____ an effort to forget the incident.

5. But when Charles _____ angry, it's hard for him to calm down.

6. It _____ him a long time to get over these things.

THINK AND SPEAK

Describe the people and the things in the picture. Try to use at least two adjectives in each sentence. Be sure to say the adjectives in the correct order.

EX.   **It's a cold, snowy day. Some people are standing near a big white house...**

VOCABULARY EXPANSION

The suffixes **-ness** and **-ment**

Notice the meaning and formation of these words.

Ann is a volunteer at the hospital, so she receives no **payment** for her work. Seeing people suffer causes her **sadness**, but helping them brings her **happiness**.

Nowadays there is a **movement** towards volunteerism. Some people, however, aren't in total **agreement** with this trend. They feel the government should spend more money on human services. They shouldn't depend on the **goodness** of a few people.

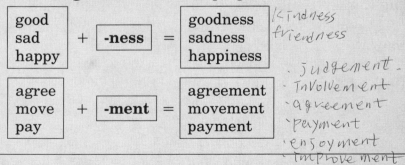

good sad happy	+	**-ness**	=	goodness sadness happiness
agree move pay	+	**-ment**	=	agreement movement payment

kindness
friendness

- *judgement*
- *Involvement*
- *agreement*
- *payment*
- *enjoyment*
- *Improvement*

The suffix **-ness** means "the state or concept of being (something), a quality." *state of being.*

The suffix **-ment** means "the act or fact of."

PRACTICE

Complete the story by filling in the suffix *-ment* or *-ness* in the blanks.

Ms. Ortiz had worked for the establish _____ only twenty years, but her retire _____ date was approaching. At 65, she still felt young and energetic. She knew it would take a new person years to match her skillful _____ on the job. Still, the manage _____ did not make many exceptions to its retire _____ policy. She knew about the president's firm _____ in his decisions, so she could only hope that his fair _____ might make a difference in his plans regarding her.

"Come in, Ms. Ortiz, come in," said the president cordially. "I've been wanting to talk with you."

"Thank you," said Ms. Ortiz. She liked his friendli _____, but it didn't affect her nervous _____ as she sat down.

"Ms. Ortiz, we've been reviewing our personnel policies," said the president. "And we've found that our mandatory retire _____ policy is both wasteful and costly. We'd like you to stay on. Will you consider it?"

"Y—Yes, thank you," she said with a small smile. His frank _____ and open _____ pleased her. "You know that I've liked working here very much. But I need a little time to decide. I'll let you know tomorrow."

"That's fine. I hope you'll decide you're in agree _____ with our new policy. It's an improve _____ over the old one."

PRONOUNCE

Final consonant clusters and third person singular verbs ending in [-s] and [-z]

[-ps]	[-ts]	[-ks]	[-fs]	[-bz]
stops	notes	likes	laughs	cabs
helps	states	takes	coughs	verbs
[-dz]	[-θs]	[-ðz]	[-gz]	[-vz]
friends	myths	clothes	dogs	adjectives
birds	breaths	breathes	legs	shelves
[-rz]	[-lz]	[-mz]	[-nz]	[-ŋz]
others	girls	comes	means	things
cars	travels	games	opens	sings

A. Listen to the words. On a sheet of paper, write 1 if you hear a final [s] sound and 2 if you hear a final [z] sound.

1. flames	5. chiefs	9. feelings	13. logs
2. bells	6. parks	10. paints	14. clubs
3. heats	7. demands	11. jokes	15. fills
4. breathes	8. drives	12. means	16. makes

B. Listen to this saying and repeat it.

Charles loves Bill's jokes. Whenever Bill tells one, Charles laughs and laughs, until it hurts. But Bill never stops saying funny things. He likes to make his friends laugh.

C. Listen to this saying and repeat it.

Nothing ever comes to pass without a cause.

CONVERSATION

Choosing a Career

Julius and Rose are friends at the university. They're discussing their plans for the future.

JULIUS: What are you going to do when you graduate?

ROSE: I don't know yet. I'm thinking about applying to medical school. They say that doctors are paid very well.

JULIUS: That's not a very good reason for going into medicine.

ROSE: What's the right reason for becoming a doctor?

JULIUS: To help other people.

ROSE: I don't mind helping people. But money's an important

consideration in choosing a career.

JULIUS: Medicine just isn't your calling. If it were, you wouldn't even

think about the money.

ROSE: First you have to think about yourself. Then you can worry

about other people. What are you going to do?

JULIUS: I've always been interested in banking.

Answer and Discuss

1. What does Rose <u>want to</u> do after college? *medical school*
2. Why does she want to be a doctor?
3. What's the right reason for becoming a doctor, according to Julius?
4. How does Rose feel about helping other people? *she to help people / doesn't mind*
5. How does she feel about money? *important consideration mind*
6. According to Julius, is medicine Rose's calling? Why not? *no*
7. Do you agree with Rose's comment, "First you have to think about *about the money* yourself"? *agree. He just thinking about / He wants carrer*
8. What does Julius want to be? *banking*
9. How do you think Rose reacted to Julius's statement, "I've always been interested in banking"?
10. How did you react to his statement?

INTERACTION

A. Discuss the following questions with a partner or with the class.

1. What are the most important reasons for choosing an occupation or profession?
2. What occupations or professions perform the greatest services for people?
3. Are there professions that don't benefit anyone?
4. How did you choose your profession? If you haven't chosen one yet, how will you choose a profession?

B. Interview another student about his or her current or future profession. Find out why the student chose that profession. Then report what you learned to the class.

STUDY 1

The passive construction: *Doctors are paid very well.*

Notice the change from object to subject.

ACTIVE: People pay | **doctors** | very well.

PASSIVE: | **Doctors** | are paid very well (by) people.

Notice the changes in the verbs.

Doctors | **help** | people. → People | **are helped** | by doctors.

A doctor | **saved** | my life. → My life | **was saved** | by a doctor.

A doctor | **is going to examine** | me next week.

→ I | **'m going to be examined** | by a doctor next week.

The object of an active sentence becomes the subject of a passive sentence. The subject of an active sentence (also called the "agent") sometimes becomes the object of the preposition **by** in the passive sentence.

The passive form of a verb consists of the same tense of the verb **be** + the past participle of the verb.

Notice the absence of the agent.

Chemistry is taught at the university **by professors.**
Chemistry is taught at the university.
My purse was stolen **by someone** during chemistry class.
My purse was stolen during chemistry class.

The agent is often not stated when it is clear from the context or when it is not known.
In the passive expression **be born,** the agent (**by one's mother**) is never used.

> **I was born** in a very small town.

P. P영 build의
세우다. 건축하다.

PRACTICE

A. Change these sentences to the passive. Drop the agent when appropriate.

EX. People all over the world know the Taj Mahal.
▷ **The Taj Mahal is known all over the world.**
      ~~Subj~~   ~~verb~~   ~~Obj~~

누구지 12에 주땔 by를 둬나.
누구인지 둥오하지 않을 때 안 넘나.

1. Shah Jahan of India built the Taj Mahal.
▷ *The Taj Mahal was built by S.J of India*

2. He chose a site in north central India.
▷

3. He hired architects from all over his empire.
▷ *Architects from all over his empire were hired.*

4. Workers laid the first stone in 1632.
▷ *The first stone was laid in 1632.*

5. Workers used pink sandstone for the outside.
▷ *Pink sandstone was used for the outside.*

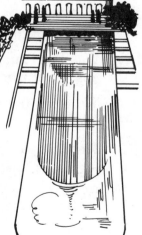

6. They put white marble on the inside.
▷

7. They finished the Taj Mahal twenty years later.
▷

8. People will always admire the Taj Mahal.
▷

9. Today, people consider the Taj Mahal to be one of the most beautiful buildings in the world.
▷

B. Answer these questions with complete sentences according to the picture.

EX. Was Paul surprised by the party?
  ▷ **Yes. Paul was surprised by the party.**

1. Were ten friends invited to the party?
  ▷ *No. five friends were invited to the party.*

2. Was the party held inside Paul's house?
  ▷ *No*   *party held => 야다. 개최하다* —— *outside*
  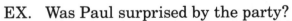
      ─. 어저다다(열리다).

3. Were balloons hung from the tree?
  ▷ *매다ᵇ hange 의 P-P*

4. Was cake served at the party?
  ▷ *제공되었다 제바다 … 에게 봉사하다*
      제공하다

5. Were candles put on the cake?
  ▷

6. Was music played at the party?
  ▷ *Yes. Music was played at the party?*

C. Ask another student these questions.

1. When were you born?
2. Where were you born?
3. Where were your parents born?
4. What language is spoken in your home? → *Korean is spoken in my country*
5. What languages are spoken in your country?
6. What products are manufactured in your country? →
7. What crops are grown in your country? →
8. What sports are played in your country? → *In my country soccer, ball are played.*

STUDY 2

Adjectives ending in -ing and -ed:
I've always been interested in banking. Banking is interesting.

Notice the difference in the meaning of adjectives ending in **-ing** and those ending in **-ed.**

Houdini's magic tricks were **fascinating.**
I've always been **fascinated** by Houdini.

Houdini's escapes were **amazing.**
People were **amazed** by his escapes.

I saw an **interesting** movie about Houdini.
I was very **interested** in the story of his life.

Craig also saw the movie, but he thought it was **boring.**
He was **bored** during the whole movie.

Craig's reaction was very **surprising.**
I was very **surprised** by his reaction.

Adjectives ending in **-ing** have the meaning of "causing a reaction or feeling." Adjectives ending in **-ed** refer to "experiencing a reaction or feeling."

Houdini's escapes **were amazing (caused amazement).**
People **were amazed (experienced amazement)** as they watched.

PRACTICE

Fill in each blank with an adjective ending in *-ed* or *-ing* formed with the verb in parentheses.

EX. Last night we were _tired_ of card games, so we went to the movies. (tire)

1. We saw *The Amazing Houdini,* and I must admit that I was truly _____. (amaze)
2. His life was very _____. (interest)
3. Everyone in the audience was _____ by the movie. (fascinate)
4. There wasn't a _____ moment in the whole movie. (bore)
5. The audience was _____ by Houdini's ability to escape from impossible situations. (mystify)
6. Some of his tricks were actually _____. (frighten)
7. People were very _____ when some spiritualists claimed that both they and Houdini had supernatural powers. (surprise)
8. Houdini knew that their claims were false, and because of the controversy, he was _____ to write the book *A Magician Among the Spirits*, which explained his tricks. (inspire)
9. People found this book _____. (fascinate)
10. Everyone was _____ when Houdini died accidentally after a public performance in 1926. (shock)

LISTEN

A. Listen carefully to the information. Then choose the statement that is true according to the information you have heard.

1. a. Anna is not a doctor.
    b. Anna's doctor is like her father.
    c. Anna's father is a doctor.

2. a. Lee lost his job.
    b. Lee's boss told him to leave.
    c. Lee is going to work at another company.

3. a. They want to tell her the bad news now.
    b. They don't want to tell her the bad news now.
    c. They told her the bad news before.

4. a. The speech began at 9:15.
    b. The speech began at 9:00.
    c. The speech began at 8:45.

5. a. Sam is working hard to get a raise.
    b. Sam doesn't want a raise.
    c. Sam won't get a raise.

6. a. The flight will probably arrive on time.
    b. The flight will probably arrive early.
    c. The flight will probably arrive late.

B. Listen carefully to the information. Then choose the correct answer.

1. a. In a train station.
    b. In a car.
    c. On a ship.

2. a. In a supermarket.
    b. In a restaurant.
    c. In a home.

3. a. This afternoon.
    b. Tomorrow morning.
    c. Tomorrow afternoon.

4. a. The ones that were given in the morning.
    b. The ones that were given in the afternoon.
    c. The ones that were given in the evening.

READ

Justice

A. Old Mrs. Sloan's body had been found at the foot of the stairs early Sunday morning by her loyal butler Wilson. She had been pushed down the stairs, but the fall did not cause *result* her death.

Now Inspector Russell of Scotland Yard was patiently interviewing all the people who had been in the house the night of the death.

"Dr. Cannon, was Mrs. Sloan a healthy woman?"

"Yes, for a woman her age, she was. She had had a heart attack, so she had to be careful. But she loved to work in her garden, and she entertained a lot."

"Wilson, do you know if Mrs. Sloan had any enemies?" *don't get along*

"Goodness, no, sir. She was loved by everyone in the community. And nobody deserved the devotion more. Mrs. Sloan always contributed generously to the local charities. And she was active in community affairs."

"Do you have any idea why Mrs. Sloan decided to change her will only last week and leave most of her estate to charity?"

"I don't know, sir."

"Mr. Sloan, as your aunt's closest relation, did you expect a larger share of your aunt's estate than the small amount you were given?"

"Frankly, yes. But nothing my aunt did surprised me."

"Why do you say that?"

"Because she was a strong-willed woman who was always changing her mind."

"What is your profession, Mr. Sloan?"

"Oh, finance. Investments, that sort of thing." ~~Kind of thing~~

"Miss Allighetti, when did you last see Mrs. Sloan...alive?"

Carla Allighetti began to cry, but she soon got control of herself.

"Saturday night, about eleven o'clock at night. I took her milk and crackers. She seemed O.K. and acted normally."

"Miss Allighetti, do you share Wilson's view of Mrs. Sloan's popularity in the village?"

The words came out loud and clear.

"No. She was a witch. She deserved to die."

Answer and Discuss

1. Did Mrs. Sloan die by falling down the stairs?
2. How was Mrs. Sloan's health, according to her doctor?
3. What did the community think of Mrs. Sloan, according to Wilson?
4. What change did Mrs. Sloan make in her will?
5. Why wasn't Philip Sloan surprised by the change in her will?
6. Who do you think Carla Allighetti is?
7. What does Carla Allighetti think of Mrs. Sloan?

B. Shortly afterward, a hearing was held to determine the circumstances of Mrs. Sloan's death. Inspector Russell was questioning the house guests again.

"Dr. Cannon, is this your signature on a prescription for 150 grams of a well-known tranquilizer?"

"Well, it certainly looks like my signature. Mrs. Sloan sometimes had nervous attacks, and I prescribed it for her."

"Dr. Cannon, we have proof that you prescribed large amounts of tranquilizers regularly for Mrs. Sloan."

"Why...why...that's outrageous!"

"Wilson, isn't it true that Mrs. Sloan had to be helped out of bed every morning because of her drugged condition?"

"Of course not. She was a strong, healthy woman."

"Miss Allighetti, isn't it true that you are really Mrs. Philip Sloan and that Mrs. Sloan objected to your marriage?"

"How did you find out? Yes, it's true. She was a proud, cruel woman. She was happy for me to be her maid, but not a member of the family! Philip and I had to keep our marriage a secret because Philip had made some bad investments and needed the inheritance to pay some debts. But she found an Italian newspaper report of our marriage and changed her will. But I didn't kill her, and neither did Philip!"

"Wilson, do you have any idea how Mrs. Sloan happened to see the Italian newspaper reporting the marriage of Mr. Sloan and Miss Allighetti?"

"Why, no. I have no idea."

"There is a newsdealer on Bond Street who remembers your asking about Italian newspapers of a specific date."

"No, that's impossible!"

"Did you not learn of the marriage from other servants and see it as a fine opportunity to safely get rid of Mrs. Sloan by throwing suspicion on Mr. Sloan and his wife? And did you not want to get rid of Mrs. Sloan because she had discovered that those prescriptions so kindly provided by Dr. Cannon were being filled and used not by her, but by *you*, and that you had even begun to forge the prescriptions?"

"Yes, yes, I had to do it. She was going to go to the police. I begged her not to, but she wouldn't listen. I had to do it."

Answer and Discuss

1. Why did Dr. Cannon say he prescribed tranquilizers for Mrs. Sloan?
2. Did he admit prescribing large amounts of tranquilizers for her?
3. Does Wilson believe that Mrs. Sloan was often drugged?
4. What was Carla Allighetti's secret?
5. Why did Philip and Carla keep their marriage a secret?
6. How did Mrs. Sloan find out about it?
7. How did the Italian newspaper probably get into Mrs. Sloan's house?
8. Who killed Mrs. Sloan? Why?
9. How do you think he killed her?

PHRASAL VERBS

Keep back, keep up with, and speak up

Notice the meaning of these phrasal verbs.

Rose was sick for a week. She was able to **keep up with** the class by studying at home. She wasn't afraid to **speak up** when the English teacher asked questions. She didn't like to **keep back** her opinions.

Keep back (separable) means "refuse to tell or give" (something).
Keep up means "continue to progress." It does not take a direct object. However, when **with** is added, it takes a direct object.
Keep up with is nonseparable.
Speak up means "speak without hesitation or fear." It does not take a direct object.

PRACTICE

Complete the sentences using the correct form of an appropriate verb from the following list.

keep	keep up	speak
keep back	keep up with	speak up

The company president called a general meeting to _____ speak _____ about an important problem: Employees weren't _____ keep back _____ their work. The president asked the employees to suggest ways to solve the problem. Most of the employees knew why they couldn't _____ keep up _____. They were simply given too much work. But not one person _____. They realized that if you want to _____ your job, sometimes it's best to _____ speak _____ your opinions at large meetings, and wait for a good opportunity to _____ directly with your boss.

THINK AND SPEAK

What are the professions of the people in these illustrations? Why do you think people choose these particular professions? Which of these people performs the greatest public service through his or her profession? Which profession do you like the best? Which do you like the least?

1.

2.

3.

4.
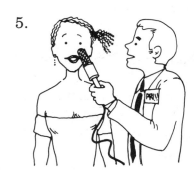

5.

6.

VOCABULARY EXPANSION

Nouns with the suffix **-ion**

Notice the meaning and formation of these words.

Last year the drama class at Washington Community College received **permission** to produce a school play. The success of this **production** led to the **creation** of a permanent theater group and caused an **explosion** of interest in drama at the college.

There was some **opposition** to the group in the beginning. Some felt that the **addition** of another student **organization** would demand too much faculty **participation**. Many professors were already overworked because of a **reduction** in staff due to a lack of money. Other faculty members felt that students already had too many **distractions** and that there should be more **concentration** on academics.

The majority of the faculty, however, saw the group as an **extension** of the literature program and hoped for the **inclusion** of plays by Shakespeare and other great playwrights. The office of **admissions** felt the theater group would attract more students to the college, and their **prediction** was correct. The new theater group was the only **explanation** for the sudden increase in students the following year.

Many verbs ending in **-ate** and **-ct** form nouns ending in **-ion**.

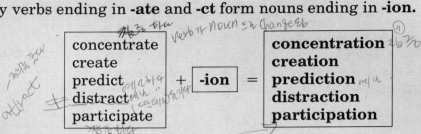

concentrate create predict distract participate	+	**-ion**	=	**concentration** **creation** **prediction** **distraction** **participation**

Many verbs ending in **-mit** form nouns ending in **-ssion**.

admit permit	+	**-ssion**	=	**admission** **permission**

Many verbs ending in **-nd** or **-de** form nouns ending in **-sion**.

extend include explode	+	**-sion**	=	**extension** **inclusion** **explosion**

Many verbs ending in **-ce** drop the **e** and add **-tion**.

produce reduce	+	**-tion**	=	**production** **reduction**

Some verbs form nouns ending in **-ition**.

add oppose	+	**-ition**	=	**addition** **opposition**

Other verbs form nouns ending in **-ation**.

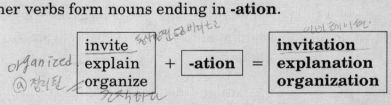

invite explain organize	+	**-ation**	=	**invitation** **explanation** **organization**

The suffix **-ion** changes verbs to nouns with the meaning "act or result of."

The heaviest stress is on the syllable preceding **-ion**.

PRACTICE

Complete the words in each paragraph with the appropriate noun ending: *-ion*, *-ssion*, *-sion*, *-tion*, *-ition*, or *-ation*.

THE WORST PROBLEM IN TODAY'S WORLD IS THE CON-

El peor problema del mundo hoy en día

The translat_____ and interpret_____ of works and speeches from one language to another takes great skill. It also takes great dedicat_____ and many years of practice for a person to be comfortable with translating and interpreting. A good translator has to know two languages to perfect_____.

I plan to attend a special school so I can become a professional translator and interpreter. Admi_____ to such a school is very difficult. I should have sent my school records last week, but I received an exten_____ of five days. The first course I have to take is a brief introduc_____ to the art of translation. The instructor's permi_____ is necessary to take it. We will be given an explan_____ of what translation and interpretation are. Their defin_____ are basically the same except that interpretation is oral, while translation is written. At the end of the year, we will receive an invit_____ to the United Nations. It will be interesting to watch the interpreters' participat_____ in the session.

PRONOUNCE

Final consonant clusters with regular past and past participle forms ending in [-t] and [-d]

[-pt]	[-kt]	[-ft]	[-st]
overslept	liked	left	crossed
stopped	talked	laughed	embarrassed
[-čt]	[-št]	[-bd]	[-gd]
watched	finished	robbed	begged
patched	wished	described	hugged
[-vd]	[-zd]	[-ǰd]	[-ðd]
arrived	closed	judged	breathed
received	proposed	urged	clothed
[-md]	[-nd]	[-ld]	[-rd]
seemed	opened	called	remembered
dreamed	happened	revealed	considered

A. Listen to the words as your teacher pronounces them. Then on a separate piece of paper, write 1 if you hear a final [d] sound and 2 if you hear a final [t] sound.

1. liked
2. closed
3. breathed
4. remembered
5. seemed
6. crossed
7. laughed
8. received
9. called
10. wished
11. begged
12. opened
13. talked
14. stopped
15. watched
16. sailed

B. Listen to this saying and repeat it.

When Friday comes on the thirteenth of the month, it's supposed to be unlucky. I was worried about my test on Friday the thirteenth. When I finished studying and closed the book, I believed I'd learned and remembered what was important. During the test, I found that my mind was clear and that I hadn't misjudged the difficulty of the exam. A week later the professor told me I'd passed. First, I smiled; then I jumped and laughed and clapped my hands. I called my best friend and told him what had happened on Friday the thirteenth.

CONMVERSATION

Honesty or Loyalty?

Kenny and Juan are on the same basketball team. Tonight they're
playing an important game that they really want to win. But Kenny has
just tripped Arthur, a player on the other team, and Arthur has fallen
down. Arthur calls a foul, but the referee doesn't blow the whistle.

ARTHUR: Foul! He tripped me. Foul!

KENNY: I didn't trip you. You slipped.

JUAN: You did trip him. I saw it. You did it on purpose.

139

KENNY: You keep out of this. You didn't see what happened. You were looking the other way.

JUAN: I was right here and I saw everything.

KENNY: Whose team are you on, anyway? If you don't keep quiet, we'll lose this game for sure.

JUAN: I wouldn't feel right if we won by cheating.

KENNY: Are you calling me a cheater? Who do you think you are?

JUAN: I'm not calling you anything. I'm just saying that you committed a foul. And you committed fouls in the last two quarters, too.

KENNY: Shut up! No one asked your opinion about this.

Answer and Discuss

1. What made Arthur fall down?
2. Who saw Kenny trip Arthur?
3. Why is Kenny furious with Juan?
4. Why does Kenny want Juan to keep quiet about the foul?
5. Why doesn't Juan want to keep quiet about it?
6. What would you do if you were Juan?
7. How would you feel if you were Kenny?
8. Tell the story as if you were Arthur.

INTERACTION

A. Read the following situation. Then, with a partner, play one of the roles described.

A department store clerk has just given a customer $10 too much in change.

1. You are the customer. You want to take the money and not say anything about it. You think the prices in the department store are too high, anyway.
2. You are a friend of the customer. You noticed the clerk's mistake. Try to persuade your friend to return the extra change. You think the clerk will be charged for the missing $10 at the end of the day when the money is counted.

B. Read the following situation. Then, with a partner, play one of the roles described.

A student cheats on an important exam by copying answers from a classmate's paper. The student is a basketball player. He will not be able to play on the school team if he fails the exam.

1. You noticed the cheating, and you want to report it to the teacher.
2. You noticed the cheating, too. But you are a friend of the basketball player. Try to persuade the other student not to report the cheating to the teacher.

STUDY 1

The order of ordinal and cardinal numbers:
You committed fouls in the last two quarters, too.

Notice the position of the ordinal and cardinal numbers.

| The | first
next
last | two
three
few | exercises were difficult. |

Ordinal numbers precede cardinal numbers. **Next** and **last** act like ordinal numbers. Quantity expressions like **few** act like cardinal numbers.

You can omit the noun modified by the numbers if it is already known.

Most of the exercises were easy, but the **first two** were difficult.

 # PRACTICE

Complete the following sentences with cardinal and ordinal numbers according to the information given.

EX. The <u>first</u> <u>three</u> swimmers competed in the freestyle event.

1. The <u>second</u> <u>three</u> swimmers competed in the butterfly.
2. The <u>third</u> <u>three</u> swimmers competed in the backstroke event.
3. The <u>fourth</u> <u>five</u> swimmers swam the breaststroke.
4. The _____ _____ finishing times in the freestyle were the same.
5. The _____ _____ finishing times in the butterfly were the same.
6. The first finishing time in the backstroke established a new record. The _____ _____ didn't.
7. The _____ _____ finishing times in the breaststroke event were the same.
8. The _____ _____ times were different.

STROKE	SWIMMERS	TIME
freestyle	Manuel John Roland	1:53 1:54 1:54
butterfly	Vera Lucy Eve	2:16 2:16 2:24
backstroke	Max Roberto Charles	2:03 2:09 2:10
breaststroke	Nobuko Elizabeth Jean Rosa Margaret	2:40 2:42 2:44 2:44 2:44

STUDY 2

The order of numbers and other adjectives:
The two best players on the team are Kenny and Juan.

Notice the position of the modifiers.

The | two | tallest | players on the team are Kenny and Juan.

Kenny is the tallest, and Juan is the | second | tallest | one .

There are | three | shorter | players who usually play with them.

The | three | shorter | ones | aren't as good as Kenny and Juan.

The number usually precedes other adjectives. *ex) That one.*
The noun can be replaced by **one** or **ones** to avoid repetition.

(*The Number before adjectives.*)

PRACTICE

Complete each sentence using a number and <u>the superlative</u> form of the adjective in parentheses.

Mr. and Mrs. Olsen came to the United States from Sweden five years ago. They have four children: Paul, 22; Marianne, 19; Greta, 14; and Hans, 10.

EX.   The <u>**two most attractive**</u> children are Marianne and Hans. (attractive)

1. The _____ musicians are Paul and Greta. (good)
2. The _____ ones are Marianne and Hans. (athletic)
3. The _____ children attended school in Sweden, but Hans didn't. (old)
4. The _____ children, Greta and Hans, speak only English. (young)
5. The _____ ones are Marianne and Greta. (bright)

STUDY 3

Sentences with an **if** condition:
We can win the game if everyone keeps quiet.

Notice the meaning of these sentences.

MAIN CLAUSE: CONDITION: · Both present tense.
                                                              · Generally True

You can play well | **if** | you practice a lot.
Can you play well | **if** | you don't practice? No, you can't.
Practice a lot | **if** | you want to play well.

Use **if** to connect a condition to the main clause. **If** conditions can be
  connected to statements, questions, and requests.
The present tense is used in the main clause and in the **if** condition
  to talk about things that are generally true.
When the **if** condition precedes the main clause, separate it with a
  comma.

> **If** you practice a lot, you **can** play well.

가정 condition 이 완료문이다

PRACTICE

Answer the questions from your own experience.

EX. What do you do if you have a headache?
     I rest for a while if I have a headache.

1. What should you eat if you want to be healthy?
    I eat Vegetable.

2. Where do you go if you want to exercise?

3. How should you dress if you want to go dancing?
    if   I wear sexy dress.

4. Who do you talk to if you feel sad?

5. What can you do if you want to stop smoking?

6. What can you do if you want to lose weight?

• What can you do (If) you have a flat tire
• what do you say (If) you caught with matches?

STUDY 4

Sentences with an **if condition** in the present tense and a main clause in the future tense:

If you don't keep quiet, we'll lose this game.

Notice the use of the tenses.

KENNY: (If you **don't keep** quiet, we**'ll lose** this game.)
JUAN: If you **cheat** again, I**'ll tell** the referee.
KENNY: If you **tell** the referee, none of the team members **will**
         ever **speak** to you again.

The future tense is used in the main clause to talk about specific
things that will happen if a certain condition is met.
When the future tense is used in the main clause, the present tense
is used in the **if** condition.

If you don't get a haircut, you'll look like a mop.

🎦 PRACTICE

Answer these questions according to the pictures.

EX. If they go out to eat tonight, where will they go?
▷ **If they go out to eat tonight, they'll go to a**
    Chinese restaurant. →Not at home

1. If they go to a restaurant, how
    much money will they spend?
▷

2. If they take a vacation this year, where will they go?
▷

The silent treatment ⟹ 말없는 처대와 니반응 (타함음CCI)
⟹ You don't answer.

3. If they go to Japan, how will they go?

▷

4. If it snows this weekend, what will you do?

▷

5. If it rains this weekend, what will you do?

▷

6. If we go to the movies tonight, what will we see?

▷

7. If we have time after the movie, where will we go?

▷

8. If we go to a café, what will we order?

▷

"에서 if가 dream 아니면 not true거

Factual( ) 문장에 could를 쓰고
can을 쓴다 could를 쓰고 would를 쓴다 (Karen)
on에서 won't를 않으면 ... 과거로 과거에서 현재 ... 의미 쓴다

STUDY 5

Contrary-to-fact conditional sentences in the present tense:
I wouldn't feel right if we won by cheating.

Notice the relation between the factual sentences and the contrary-
to-fact conditional sentences.

many(true)

FACTUAL: *(fact)*

CONTRARY-TO-FACT CONDITIONAL: *opp. dream, imagination*

The weather isn't nice.
Susan won't go to the beach.

If the weather **were** nice,
Susan **would go** to the beach.

Susan doesn't have any money.
She can't go to the movies.

If Susan **had** some money,
she **could go** to the movies.

past → means present

Susan doesn't feel happy today.
She won't go visit Mary.

If Susan **felt** happy today,
she**'d go** visit Mary.

If + past

would + infinitive → 진행형으로도(?)
could

To form the contrary-to-fact conditional sentences in the present
tense, use the conditional **would** (or **could**) + the simple form of
the verb in the main clause. Use the past tense in the **if** clause.
Were is usually used instead of **was** with **I, he, she,** and **it** in the
if clause. *ex), If I were a fish, I'd live in the ocean.*

The use of these tenses indicates that the condition of the **if** clause is
not true. *· If my brother were here, he'd cook for me*

The contraction of **would** is **'d.**

(X) the weather were
it was
I, he, she, it = were
was가 이렇게 were

PRACTICE

**Make contrary-to-fact conditional sentences using the information
given in the sentence pairs below.**

EX. I don't have enough money. I can't buy a
new tape.

▷ **If I had enough money, I could buy a new
tape.**

FACTUAL

can't vary to fact

① ex I don't have a car.
I can't drive to the store.

If I had a car.
I could drive to the store.

(handwritten top notes)
- If you were an animal, what would you be?
- If you were invisible, what would you do?
  - 주제 ~에 관해서 말하는 것
- conversation

1. Robert has to work this weekend. He won't go to the mountains.
   ▷

(handwritten) to be 있다 always were —

2. I don't have a good job. I can't afford a nice car.
   ▷ *(handwritten)* If I had a good job
   I could afford a nice car
   (above "afford" handwritten: pay)

(handwritten right) 돈이 충분히 있다
"Wha's afford mean?"

3. I don't have a car. I can't drive to the ocean.
   ▷ *(handwritten)* had   would

4. It isn't raining. I won't stay indoors.
   ▷ *(handwritten)* If were raining. I would stay to indoors.

5. She doesn't have time. She won't do the dishes.
   ▷

6. Jane is sick. She won't go to work today.
   ▷ *(handwritten)* If Jane were sick

7. Mr. Chui has no money. He can't take a vacation.
   ▷

(handwritten bottom)
The weather stincks   If the weather were
I won't go out   I would go out

LISTEN

A. Listen carefully to the information. Then choose the statement that is true according to the information you have heard.

1. a. John reads more slowly than his friends.
   b. John's friends read as fast as he does.
   c. John reads faster than his friends.

2. a. This car is more dangerous than other cars.
   b. This car is safer than other cars.
   c. This car is cheaper than other cars.

3. a. Anita drives twice as fast as Robert.
   b. Anita drives half as fast as Robert.
   c. Robert can drive to Miami in two hours, too.

4. a. They deliver the mail on holidays.
   b. They won't deliver the mail today.
   c. They will deliver the mail today.

5. a. It's too late to call my parents.
   b. It's late enough for me to call my parents.
   c. It's early, so I'm not going to call my parents.

6. a. Barbara earns $600 a month.
   b. Barbara earns $900 a month.
   c. Barbara earns $300 a month.

B. Listen carefully to the information. Then choose the correct answer.

1. a. In New York.
   b. In Washington, D.C.
   c. In Atlanta.

2. a. The sports section.
   b The front page.
   c. Different sections.

3. a. At the office.
   b. On a trip.
   c. At the State Department.

4. a. At a doctor's office.
   b. At a supermarket.
   c. At a school.

READ

Lost

A. Finally, Ron admitted to himself that he was lost. He realized he could no longer hear the other hikers' voices. He changed direction, shouting their names. Still no voices. He was completely lost.

Ron sat down to think about what he should do. It was beginning to get dark, and he didn't want to wander around the forest at night, getting farther away from the camp. He decided he should stay where he was, at least until the next morning. He was hungry, but there was only a small piece of candy in his pocket. He ate it and then made a bed of leaves beside a log and lay down to try to sleep. His coat wasn't very warm, and the cold kept him awake for a long time. He covered himself with more leaves and finally fell asleep.

The next morning, he woke up early. He tried shouting for the others again, but there was no answer. Then he started walking. After some time, he sat down to think again. If he could build a fire, someone might see the smoke and find him. But how could he build a fire without matches or even a knife? He found some sticks and small pieces of wood, but they were all wet. When he tried rubbing them together to start a fire, they just broke into smaller pieces.

Answer and Discuss

1. How did Ron realize that he was lost in the forest?
2. What did he do when he realized he was lost?
3. How did Ron spend the night in the forest?
4. Why did Ron try to build a fire the next day?
5. How did he try to build a fire? What happened?

B. By Saturday afternoon, Ron was very hungry. He began walking and soon found a small stream. He stopped to take a drink. Suddenly, he stared at the stream, trying to remember something he had read about finding your way out of a forest. Something about following a stream... That was it! You were supposed to follow a stream in the direction it was flowing, and it would lead you to a road, town, or city. Ron began to follow the water downstream.

It was almost noon on Saturday when Ron's friends reached the ranger station. They told the rangers about Ron, and a search party was organized immediately. By three o'clock, the first group of searchers had begun looking for Ron. Each group carried compasses, maps, medicine, and a radio. Meanwhile the state police sent two people in a traffic helicopter to search the forest from the air. Ron's parents arrived at the ranger station at three-thirty with another group of state police.

The rangers wanted to find Ron before nightfall. He had already spent one night out in the rough terrain, and the weather prediction for Saturday night was freezing temperatures and possible rain. It began to get dark. At about midnight, after the last group of searchers had returned to the ranger station, another truck arrived. It was carrying four state police officers and some bloodhounds. Since the dogs could pick up Ron's trail using their sense of smell, they didn't need to wait for daylight. The state police decided to begin searching right away.

Answer and Discuss

1. What did Ron do to find his way out of the forest?
2. How did the rangers find out that Ron was lost?
3. What did the rangers do to help?
4. Why did they want to find Ron before nightfall?
5. How was it possible for the state police to continue the search after dark?

C.   After following the stream for a long time, Ron noticed that it was beginning to get dark again. He would have to spend another night out in the forest. It seemed to be colder, too. He decided he should build himself a shelter for the night. He found a very large log near the stream. Then he laid one end of a smaller log on top of it and the other end on the ground. This left a small space between the small log and the ground—just enough room to crawl under. He continued laying logs this way until he had made a shelter long enough to lie under. Then he put some leaves on top of it and placed more logs, sticks, and leaves at one end to keep out any wind. After taking a drink from the stream, he climbed inside his shelter and tried to fall asleep.

It was raining when Ron woke up. He stayed inside his shelter, trying to stay as dry as possible. Suddenly, he heard a noise. It sounded very far away. He couldn't tell what it was at first, but it seemed to be coming closer. It sounded like dogs—barking dogs. Ron jumped up and began to shout as loudly as he could. Soon he saw the police and dogs coming toward him following the stream.

When they had reached the ranger station, the police told Ron's parents, "Your son is a very smart young man. He would have found his way out by this afternoon. He didn't need our help at all." Just the same, Ron was very glad they found him when they did.

By Ann F. Davis

Answer and Discuss

1. How did Ron build a shelter the second night?
2. Why did he stay inside his shelter after he woke up?
3. What made Ron begin to shout as loudly as he could?
4. Why did the police say that Ron was very smart?
5. What would you do if you were lost in a forest?

PHRASAL VERBS

Keep out, look up to, and take back

No body lives there
don't come inside
Stay outside

Notice the meaning of these phrasal verbs.

The sign on the door of the abandoned house said, **"Keep Out."**
I have always **looked up to** people who can control themselves.
It takes courage to **take back** unkind remarks.

Keep out means "remain outside or uninvolved." It does not take an object. However, when **of** is added, it does take an object.
　　　I try to **keep out of** my coworkers' private lives.

Keep out (separable) can also mean "prevent entrance or involvement." With this meaning, it takes an object. **Of** can also be added in this use.
　　　Please **keep** the dog **out of** the house.

Look up to (nonseparable) means "admire."
Take back (separable) means "retract" (something).

I take back what I said.
I take it back.
Have you ever taken back
ex: Who do you look up to?
I look up to my mother.

PRACTICE

Complete the sentences using the correct form of an appropriate verb from the following list.

keep	look	take
keep out of	look up to	take back

　　After the basketball game, Kenny and Juan went back to the locker room to _____ showers and get dressed. Kenny was feeling bad about their argument. He had always _looked up to_ Juan, and he wanted to ___keep___ his friendship. Finally he ___looked___ at Juan and said, "I want to _take back_ what I said on the court. I realize that you were really being a good friend—you were just helping me to _keep out of_ trouble."

THINK AND SPEAK

Three people are waiting in line at the check-out counter of a supermarket. A boy arrives with only one item—a six-pack of soda— and wants to cut into the line. What would you do if you were the boy who wants to cut in line? What would you do if you were one of the people waiting in line? What would you do if you were the clerk at the cash register? Act out the situation with some of the other students in the class. Use the words given below the picture.

wait in line
cut into the line
go to the back of the line

be in a hurry
complain
a six-pack of soda
a shopping cart

VOCABULARY EXPANSION

The suffixes **-less** and **-ly**

Notice the meaning and formation of these words.

   The price of meat became a problem **recently**. Prices rose in a **disorderly** manner on a **weekly** basis. Some people decided to observe two **meatless** days a week. Of course, vegetarians **simply** continued their **daily** diet. Store owners couldn't believe it; they were **speechless**. But many customers continued to avoid meat **happily**. They **gladly** supported the boycott and **greatly** contributed to its success.

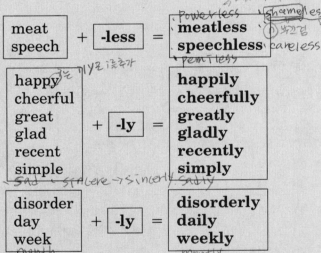

meat speech	+ **-less** =	**meatless** **speechless**

happy cheerful great glad recent simple	+ **-ly** =	**happily** **cheerfully** **greatly** **gladly** **recently** **simply**

disorder day week	+ **-ly** =	**disorderly** **daily** **weekly**

The suffix **-less** changes nouns to adjectives with the meaning "without, free from."
The suffix **-ly** changes adjectives to adverbs.
The suffix **-ly** also changes some nouns to adjectives.
The suffix **-ly** replaces adjectives ending in **-le**.
If a word ends in **y**, change the **y** to **i** before adding the suffix:

happy	+	**-ly**	=	**happily**
penny	+	**-less**	=	**penniless**

PRACTICE

**Complete the story by filling in the suffix missing from each word:
-less or -ly.**

The assistant to the president is a friend____ person with a love____ smile. She speaks soft____ but firm____. Her desk is usual ____ order____, and her reports are always written very clear____. She's never care____ in her work, and whenever anyone asks her to do something, she does it quick____ and cheerful____. She realizes it's point____ to get annoyed at others.

Recent____ she attended a business conference where she gave a lecture which left her boss speech____. Her presentation was so careful____ prepared that she easi____ kept everyone's attention.

Her year____ vacation is approaching, but she still doesn't know where she wants to go. She likes relaxed and noise____ surroundings where she can rest peaceful____, and she definite____ prefers warm places to cold ones. Last year she went to Martinique. She would glad____ return there. She still remembers her dai____ walks on the beach and the delicious meals of fish and fruit, which suited her meat____ diet. Most of all, she remembers the friend____ people. After the long workdays and some sleep____ nights during the past few weeks, she is ready to take another vacation soon.

PRONOUNCE

Consonants followed by syllabic consonants

[-Cl̩]	[-Cm̩]	[-Cn̩]
apple	mysticism	button
table	capitalism	kitten
able	rhythm	dozen
bottle		listen
little		person

A. The syllabic consonants [l̩], [m̩], and [n̩] are in unstressed syllables. Pronounce these words after your teacher before you try them alone.

1. candle	5. mysticism	9. listen
2. bottle	6. rhythm	10. fasten
3. little	7. capitalism	11. garden
4. ankle	8. prism	12. suddenly

B. Listen to this saying and repeat it.

Kittens like people. They like to rub against people's legs. They play under and over tables, bicycles, and cartons. They play with buttons, bundles, candles, pencils, and little balls of cotton.

C. Listen to this saying and repeat it.

It's like looking for a nee**dle** in a haystack.
Hasty climbers have su**dden** falls.

CONVERSATION

Getting Admitted to a University

Mortimer Crystal would like to enter an engineering school where the admissions policy is very selective. He has come to the admissions office to find out about his application.

MS. McCANN: Hello, I'm Priscilla McCann.

MORTIMER: Hello, Ms. McCann. I'm Mortimer Crystal. I mailed my application for admission four weeks ago, and I haven't heard anything yet.

MS. McCANN: I'll look for your file. Please have a seat.

MORTIMER: Thank you.

MS. McCANN: How do you spell your last name?

MORTIMER: C-r-y-s-t-a-l. Like glass.

MS. McCANN: Here it is. I'll be glad to talk to you today, but I must tell you that the admissions committee hasn't made a decision on your application yet.

MORTIMER: Do you think I'll be accepted?

MS. McCANN: It's hard to say. Your high school grade average is low.

MORTIMER: But I got good grades in math and science.

MS. McCANN: That's true.

MORTIMER: And I participated in a lot of extracurricular activities when I was in high school. I belonged to all the science clubs and I was on the track team.

MS. McCANN: (*Looking at his application*) I see that you had a job, too.

MORTIMER: Yes. I worked as an assistant in an electronics laboratory for two years. While I was working there, I decided to become an engineer.

Answer and Discuss

1. Why has Mortimer Crystal come to the Office of Admissions?
2. Has the admissions committee made a decision yet?
3. Why isn't Ms. McCann sure if Mortimer will be accepted?
4. What does Mortimer say to convince Ms. McCann that he has good qualifications?
5. Do you think that extracurricular activities are important in preparing for the university? Why or why not?
6. Do you think that Mortimer will be admitted to the engineering school? Why or why not?
7. Tell the story as if you were Mortimer. As if you were Ms. McCann.

INTERACTION

A. Read the following situation. Then, with a partner, play one of the roles described.

University X is interviewing applicants to the undergraduate program.
1. Your high-school grades are average, but they are very good in science (or English). Convince the admissions officer that you should be admitted because you want to major in a science (or English).
2. You are interviewing an applicant for admission to the undergraduate college of University X. His or her grades are only average. Try to find out as much as you can about the student's other qualifications.

B. Read the following situation. Then, with a partner, play one of the roles described.

Company X is interviewing for the positions of electrician, computer technician, computer operator, office assistant, and management trainee.
1. You would like one of the positions because they pay well and they are in a city you would like to live in. To help you in the interview, you have prepared a list of reasons why you are qualified for the job. Explain them to the interviewer.
2. You are interviewing a person for one of the positions above. Try to find out as much as possible about the person's qualifications for the job.

STUDY 1

Sentences with time clauses: *I participated in a lot of extracurricular activities when I was in high school. While I was working there, I decided to become an engineer.*

Notice the relation between the main clause and the time clause.

MAIN CLAUSE: TIME CLAUSE:

The man fell out of the car   **when** the door opened.
He fell out   **while** the car was moving.
The car stopped   **after** he fell out.
He fell out   **before** the car stopped.

When, while, after, and **before** can express time relations between
  two clauses.
When introduces an action that takes place at the same time as the
  action in the main clause.
While introduces an extended action which is in progress at the time
  of the action in the main clause.
If the time clause precedes the main clause, it is separated from it by
  a comma.
> After the man fell out of the car, the car stopped.

If the main clause is in the future tense, the time clause still must be
in the present tense, even if it refers to an action in the future.
> When I go to college, I'll study engineering.
> I'm going to have a job while I'm in college.

PRACTICE

A. Fill in the blanks with _when_, _while_, _before_ or _after_.

_____ I woke up this morning, I looked out the window and saw the cold rain. I turned over and closed my eyes again. But _____ I was dozing, the phone rang. It was my coworker. "You're late! You said you'd pick me up at eight o'clock!" I saw it was already eight-fifteen _____ I looked at the clock. I jumped out of bed and rushed to get ready for work. _____ I showered, I dressed in record time. I quickly fed the dog and cat _____ I left the house. _____ my coworker and I walked into the office, the boss looked at us and then at her watch. "_____ you put away your coats, please come and see me," she said. What a way to start the day!

B. Complete the sentences according to the pictures.

EX. Peter and his friend had an accident while

<u>**they were driving**</u> .

1. The car was turning a corner when

_____ .

2. The car traveled for fifty meters before

_____ .

3. A crowd had already formed when

_____ .

4. Peter was given first aid before

_____ .

5. After Peter was taken to the hospital,

_____ .

STUDY 2

The use of the verbs **make** and **do**:
I've done the dishes, but I haven't made dinner yet.

Notice the uses of **make** and **do**.

Make means "construct or produce something."
My brother John and I **made lunch** for the family yesterday. I
made some soup, and John **made some sandwiches**. John picked
a fight with me while we were **making lunch**. He is always **making
trouble**. He also **made a big mess** while he was **making the
sandwiches**. Father **made quite a scene** when he saw the kitchen.

Make means "cause to become."
My boss **makes** me **mad**. He **makes** my work **difficult**.

Make means "cause someone to do something."
Mortimer's parents **make** him **study** very hard.

Do means "perform some action."
What are you **doing** on Sunday?
Nothing. I don't like to **do** anything on Sundays.

Do mea_____re."
I_____Saturday. I **do the housework** in the
mo_____**some gardening**. In the afternoon
I do_____ing. I never have time to **do much
work**_____**do the cooking** and **the dishes**.

Here a_____h **do**.
I helpe_____**part**.
I did eve_____**best**.
I didn't h_____ or carry her groceries home, but I
did it anyw_____**deed**.
It's impossi_____r. Novak to stop eating butter. He can't **do
without** it.
We all liked Ms. Lyon's work. She **did a good job**.
The storm was terrible. It **did a lot of damage** to the buildings in
the town.

PRACTICE

Complete the sentences with the correct form of _make_ or _do_. Be sure to use the correct tense.

EX. Oscar <u>is going to make</u> dinner for everyone next Saturday.

1. My boss _____ us work very hard yesterday.

2. I always have to _____ a lot of work at the office.

3. The new company president _____ a lot to improve the business since she began working here.

4. The customer _____ a big scene in the restaurant because the waiter spilled coffee on him.

5. Money problems can _____ life very difficult.

6. If I _____ more money, I'd have fewer problems.

7. The hairdresser just _____ my hair, and now it's raining!

8. The plane _____ a lot of damage when it crashed into the building.

9. In our house, everyone has to help _____ the cooking.

10. When you have a cold, hot lemonade with honey really _____ your throat good.

11. Rose _____ a good deed today. She saw someone fall down in the street, and she helped him get up.

12. After I _____ my homework, I'll watch television.

13. Mortimer _____ the decision to become an engineer while he was working in an electronics laboratory.

14. When young people have nothing to _____, they sometimes _____ trouble in the streets.

LISTEN

A. Listen carefully to the information. Then choose the statement that is true according to the information you have heard.

1. a. My uncle didn't see me.
   b. My uncle saw someone who looked like me.
   c. I saw someone who looked like my uncle.

4. a. Maria's father liked her choice.
   b. Maria didn't want to study business.
   c. Maria's father didn't like her choice.

2. a. Max likes to sleep with the door open.
   b. Max likes to sleep with the door locked.
   c. Max always leaves the door closed.

5. a. Jack is not afraid to express his opinion.
   b. Jack never agrees with anything.
   c. Jack doesn't write many letters.

3. a. She had eight broken glasses.
   b. She had two broken glasses.
   c. She had six broken glasses.

6. a. Tony is at the zoo.
   b. Tony is at school.
   c. Tony is at the beach.

B. Listen carefully to the information. Then choose the correct answer.

1. a. At 10:20.
   b. At 10:30.
   c. At 10:40.

3. a. Waiter and customer.
   b. Secretary and boss.
   c. Clerk and customer.

2. a. A driver.
   b. A police officer.
   c. A detective.

4. a. In the winter.
   b. When everyone else goes.
   c. When fewer people go.

READ

Hearts and Hands

A. At Denver there was a line of passengers coming into the cars on the express train going east. In one car there sat a very pretty young woman dressed in elegant taste and surrounded by all the luxurious comforts of a frequent traveler. Among the new passengers were two men: one of good appearance with a strong, open face and manner; the other a suffering, sad-faced person of strong body and rough dress. The two were handcuffed together.

As they passed down the aisle of the car the only empty seat was one facing the attractive young woman. Here the handcuffed couple sat down. The young woman's eyes fell on them with a distant, quick look; then with a lovely smile lighting her face and a soft pink coloring her round cheeks, she held out a little hand in a gray glove. When she spoke, her voice, full, sweet, and sure, showed that she was used to speaking and being heard.

"Well, Mr. Easton, if you will make me speak first, I suppose I must. Don't you ever remember old friends when you meet them in the West?"

The younger man raised himself sharply at the sound of her voice, seemed to fight a slight confusion which he threw off quickly, and then held her fingers tightly with his left hand.

"It's Miss Fairchild," he said, with a smile. "I'll ask you to excuse the other hand; it's busy doing something else at present."

He slightly raised his right hand, held tied by the shining handcuffs to the left one of his companion. The glad look in the woman's eyes showly changed to a surprised shock. The soft pink coloring left her cheeks. Her lips opened in pained confusion.

Easton, with a little laugh, as if amused, was about to speak again when the other man stopped him. The sad-faced man had been watching the woman's face with quick glances from his sharp eyes.

"You'll excuse me for speaking, miss, but I see you know the sheriff here. If you'll ask him to speak a word for me when we get to the prison, he'll do it, and it'll make things easier for me there. He's taking me to the state prison. It's seven years for counterfeiting."

"Oh!" said the woman, with a deep breath and returning color. "So that is what you are doing out here. A sheriff!"

"My dear Miss Fairchild," said Easton, calmly, "I had to do something. Money has a way of disappearing, and you know it takes money to keep step with our group in Washington. I heard about this job in the West, and—well, a job as sheriff isn't quite as high as that of ambassador, but..."

Answer and Discuss

1. Where does the story take place?
2. What was special about the two men who got on the train at Denver?
3. Where did the two men sit down?
4. What was the name of the younger man, who had a good appearance and a strong, open face and manner?
5. Why did Miss Fairchild suddenly look shocked?
6. Why was the man going to prison?
7. Why did Miss Fairchild suddenly feel better?
8. Why did Mr. Easton compare the position of sheriff with that of ambassador?
9. What reason did Mr. Easton give for living in the West?

B. "The ambassador," said the woman, warmly, "doesn't call anymore. He needn't ever have done so. You ought to know that. And so now you are one of these lively Western heroes, and you ride and shoot and get into all kinds of danger. That's different from the Washington life. You have been missed in the old group."

The woman's eyes, opening a little, went back to rest on the shining handcuffs.

"Don't you worry about them, miss," said the other man. "All sheriffs handcuff one hand to their prisoner's to keep him from getting away. Mr. Easton knows his business."

"Will we see you again soon in Washington?" asked the woman.

"Not soon, I think," said Easton. "My butterfly days are over."

"I love the West," said the woman. Her eyes were shining softly. She looked away out of the car window. She began to speak truly and simply, without proud style and manner. "Mama and I spent the summer in Denver. She went home a week ago because Father was slightly ill. I could live and be happy in the West. I think the air here agrees with me. Money isn't everything. But people don't always understand things and they go on confused...."

"Say, Mr. Sheriff," said the sad-faced man. ["not smile"] "This isn't completely fair. I need a drink, and I haven't had a smoke all day. Haven't you talked long enough? Take me to the smoker now, won't you? I'm half-dead for a pipe."

The handcuffed passengers rose to their feet, Easton with the same slow smile on his face.

"I can't say no to a request for tobacco," he said. "It's the one friend of a man in trouble. Good-bye, Miss Fairchild. Duty calls, you know." He held out his hand for a good-bye.

"It's too bad you are not going East," she said, fixing her clothes with manner and style. "But you must go on to the prison, I suppose?"

"Yes," said Easton. "I must go on to the prison."

The two men walked down the aisle into the smoker.

The two passengers in the seat near them had heard most of the conversation. Said one of them: "That sheriff's a good fellow. Some of these Western fellows are all right."

"Very young to be a sheriff, isn't he?"

"Young!" said the first speaker, "Why—oh! Didn't you understand? Say—did you ever know a sheriff to handcuff a prisoner to his *right* hand?"

Adapted from "Hearts and Hands"
by O. Henry

Answer and Discuss

1. What is a Western sheriff's life like, according to Miss Fairchild?
2. What did Miss Fairchild say to show that she was interested in Mr. Easton?
3. Why did Mr. Easton leave Miss Fairchild and go to the smoker?
4. Why did one of the passengers who had heard the conversation say "That sheriff's a good fellow"?
5. Which man did the second passenger think was the sheriff?
6. Which of the two men was the sheriff? How do you know?

PHRASAL VERBS

Look over, fill out, and figure out

Notice the meaning of these phrasal verbs.

When you apply for a home loan, be sure to **look over** the information carefully, **fill out** the application completely, and ask the bank loan officer to **figure out** exactly how much the monthly payments will be.

Look over (separable) means "inspect or examine" (something).
Fill out (separable) means "add what is needed to make (something) complete."
Figure out (separable) means "calculate or think about until one understands" (something).

PRACTICE

Complete the sentences using the correct form of an appropriate verb from the following list.

fill out	looked over	figure out
looking	fill	looked

"Could you please _____ this application?" asked the personnel officer as she handed me a six-page form. I was _____ for a job for the first time in my life, and I was quite nervous. I _____ each page of the form carefully, then took out a pen and began to _____ it _____. An hour later I was ready for the test. The instructions were complicated, and it took me a while to _____ them _____. Finally came the actual interview. After many questions the personnel officer said, "You'll hear from me soon. I need to _____ this position immediately." As I left, I _____ at my watch. I had spent three hours there, and I had _____ the whole process would only take an hour!

THINK AND SPEAK

Describe what is happening in the picture. What questions is the interviewer asking? How will the person answer the questions? How would you answer the questions?

VOCABULARY EXPANSION

The suffixes **-er/-or** and **-able/-ible**

Notice the meaning and formation of these words.

Joy works. She is a **worker**.
Some machines compute. They're **computers**.
A company employs people. It's an **employer**.

work compute employ	+	-er	=	worker computer employer

Felipe acts. He's an **actor**.
A machine projects a film. It's a **projector**.
Linda translates French into English. She's a **translator**.

act project translate	+	-or	=	actor projector translator

I can believe it. It's **believable**.
The book isn't too difficult. It's **readable**.
I can understand it. It's **understandable**.

believe read understand	+	-able	=	believable readable understandable

I can believe it. It's **credible**.
The writing is clear. It's **legible**.
I can understand it. It's **comprehensible**.

cred- leg- comprehens-	+	-ible	=	credible legible comprehensible

The suffixes **-er/-or** form nouns with the meaning "person or thing that does something."
The suffix **-able** forms adjectives with the meaning "can be (+ passive verb)" or "is appropriate for" (something).
The variation **-ible** is used with some words of Latin origin.

PRACTICE

Complete the story using the correct form of the suffix -er/-or or -able/-ible.

I'm reading a new book by a famous science fiction writ _____, and I'm finding it very enjoy _____. Although the plot is complicated, it's very believ _____. The main character is the invent _____ of a comput _____ program that is designed to invade computers all over the world. The program is a computer "virus" that would destroy valu _____ information. It would even cause the collapse of civilization. I won't tell you the ending, but it's incred _____. Some readers have never reached the end, and that's understand _____, because the book is 600 pages long and contains a few incomprehens _____ passages.

PRONOUNCE

Because all vowels tend to become [ə] or [i] in unstressed syllables, the spelling of these unstressed vowels shows great variation.

[ə]	[i]
a across, surface, **a** e the, even o **of**, purpose u circus ou famous	i scientist, atomic, going e wanted, rises

A. **Write these words on a sheet of paper. Place an accent mark on the stressed vowel, circle the unstressed vowel, and identify the unstressed vowel as [ə] or [i].**

1. s ú r f (a) c e ___[ə]___
2. a l a r m _____
3. p r a y i n g _____
4. h a r m f u l _____
5. d e s p i t e _____

6. e n d e d _____
7. a w a y _____
8. a d m i r e _____
9. d e m a n d _____
10. r e l y _____

B. **Listen to this saying and repeat it.**

The famous atomic scientist wants to know the purpose of the experiment. Many people are going to worry about it. It should be stopped if it's very dangerous.

The circus performer jumps from the surface, floats across the stadium, and rises high into the air. Suddenly, she misses, falls through the air, and lands in a net.

IRREGULAR VERBS

VERB	PAST FORM	PAST PARTICIPLE
be	was/were	been
become	became	become
begin	began	begun
blow	blew	blown
break	broke	broken
bring	brought	brought
burst	burst	burst
buy	bought	bought
catch	caught	caught
choose	chose	chosen
come	came	come
cost	cost	cost
cut	cut	cut
do	did	done
drink	drank	drunk
drive	drove	driven
eat	ate	eaten
fall	fell	fallen
feel	felt	felt
fight	fought	fought
find	found	found
fit	fit	fit
forget	forgot	forgotten
get	got	gotten
give	gave	given
go	went	gone
grow	grew	grown
have	had	had
hear	heard	heard
hide	hid	hidden
hit	hit	hit
hold	held	held
hurt	hurt	hurt
keep	kept	kept
kneel	knelt	knelt
know	knew	known
lay	laid	laid
leave	left	left

VERB	PAST FORM	PAST PARTICIPLE
lend	lent	lent
let	let	let
lie	lay	lain
lose	lost	lost
make	made	made
meet	met	met
pay	paid	paid
put	put	put
ride	rode	ridden
ring	rang	rung
rise	rose	risen
run	ran	run
say	said	said
see	saw	seen
sell	sold	sold
set	set	set
show	showed	shown
sit	sat	sat
sing	sang	sung
sleep	slept	slept
speak	spoke	spoken
spend	spent	spent
split	split	split
stand	stood	stood
steal	stole	stolen
sting	stung	stung
swim	swam	swum
take	took	taken
teach	taught	taught
tell	told	told
think	thought	thought
throw	threw	thrown
understand	understood	understood
wake	woke	woken
wear	wore	worn
win	won	won
write	wrote	written

KEY TO PRONUNCIATION

Vowels and Diphthongs

[iy]	sh**ee**p
[i]	sh**i**p
[ey]	p**ai**n
[e]	n**e**t
[æ]	p**a**n, m**a**n
[a]	f**a**ther, s**o**cks
[ow]	ph**o**ne
[ɔ]	P**au**l, **a**ll
[uw]	p**oo**l, tw**o**
[u]	f**oo**t, p**u**ll
[ə̂]	n**u**t
[ə]	**a**cross

[ay]	b**uy**, **eye**
[aw]	m**ou**th
[ɔy]	b**oy**

Consonants

VOICELESS		VOICED	
[pʰ]	**p**an	[b]	**b**and
[tʰ]	**t**an	[d]	**d**ay
[kʰ]	**c**an	[g]	**g**ood
[f]	**f**an	[v]	**v**an
[θ]	**th**ree, ei**th**er	[ð]	**th**ey, ei**th**er
[s]	**s**ip	[z]	**z**ip
[š]	**sh**in	[ž]	lei**s**ure
[č]	**ch**in	[ǰ]	**j**am
[p]	na**p**	[l]	**l**ight
[t]	ba**t**	[r]	**r**ight
[k]	ba**ck**	[m]	so**m**e
		[n]	su**n**
		[ŋ]	su**ng**

Semiconsonants

[y]	**y**am, **y**es
[w]	**w**ood
[h]	**h**ood, **h**e

Syllabic Consonants

[l̥]	app**le**
[l̥]	stop **'em** (stop them)
[n̥]	did**n't**

Stress and Intonation

Syllable stress (within a word):

Phrase or sentence stress: ●—

Intonation levels
  4 extra high
  3 high
  2 mid
  1 low

Endings for intonation levels
  rise
  sustain
  fade out

Examples of stress and intonation

yes-no question   Is he home?

information question   Where is he?

statement   He's sleeping.

with emphasis   He's still sleeping!

VOCABULARY

These are the words introduced in Book 5. The number after each word indicates the page on which it first appears. If a word can be used as more than one part of speech, the way it is used in the text is indicated as follows: n= noun, v = verb, adj = adjective, adv = adverb, prep = preposition, and conj = conjunction. The abbreviation pl (= plural) is used to indicate a noun which is generally used in the plural form.

INDEX